The Flight Across the Ice

Patricia Clough

The Flight Across the Ice

The Escape of the East Prussian Horses

HAUS BOOKS
LONDON

Originally published in German under the title *In Langer Reihe über das Haff: Die Flucht der Trakehner aus Ostpreußen* by dtv, Munich, Germany

First published in English in Great Britain in 2009 by
Haus Publishing Limited, 70 Cadogan Place, London, SW1X 9AH

A CIP catalogue record for this book is available from the British Library

ISBN 978-1-906598-34-1

Designed and typeset in Berkeley by MacGuru Ltd
Printed and bound by J F Print Ltd
Jacket illustration courtesy Alamy Images

To Isabella and Paolo

Contents

Author's Preface

It has taken well over half a century for this story to be told. Not that the flight of the Trakehners, some of the most superb horses the world has ever known, was a secret. Nor were the terrible experiences of their guardians and owners and countless other East Prussians as they fled the advancing, and avenging, Red Army in the last months of the Second World War. They were simply the subject of a strange taboo.

After the war, as Germans tried to rebuild their lives, most preferred to blank out the horrors, the traumas and the shame. As the young West German republic sought acceptance in the world, and as its Communist neighbours branded its people who wanted their lost lands back in the east 'revanchists' and 'irredentists', the plight of the East Prussians and other refugees was something of a political embarrassment. The fact that hundreds of thousands of them had been killed or had died during the flight westward, countless others raped, imprisoned or deported, and that almost two and a half million had lost their homes and their land forever, was an inconvenient truth. No one wanted to know.

A generation had to pass before an American-made television documentary, *Holocaust,* finally broke through the psychological barrier and the German public started to talk about the war, the crimes and the guilt. But the fact that millions of Germans had also suffered and that others had also committed terrible atrocities, still felt too much to handle. No one wanted to seem to excuse German crimes by pointing out Soviet ones. Another generation – that of the grandchildren – had to grow up before this barrier could begin to crumble.

Without reckoning up degrees of guilt on either side, that terrible chapter in European history is at last being remembered and understood. The Trakehners, many East Prussians' most loved and prized possessions and their greatest asset – horses renowned throughout the world for their toughness, speed, intelligence and remarkable grace and beauty – are an integral part of that story.

Main Characters

State breeders

Ernst Ehlert, *Landstallmeister* (director) of Trakehnen, with his granddaughter Lilli and family

Martin Heling, *Landstallmeister* of Georgenburg, wife and son

Hans Seyffert, *Oberlandstallmeister* (Master of Horse) in Berlin

Friedrich Kiaulehn, head of Trakehnen hunting stables, Nazi Party boss and mayor of Trakehnen

Helmut Hufenbach and Otto Fiege, stable boys

Private breeders

Barbara von Sperber

Anna von Zitzewitz, daughter Erdmute and son

Franz Scharffetter and son Hans-Joachim

Peter Elxnat and family

Gerd Lehmann, mother and sister

Brigitte Boettcher, husband and family

Johanna Sasse, husband Karl and family

Prince Alexander zu Dohna

Fritz Schilke, head of the Trakehner Breeders' Association

Nazi officials

Erich Koch, Gauleiter of East Prussia, governor of Ukraine

Hermann Göring, various offices including Reich Marshal and Air Minister

Russians

Lev Kopelev, propaganda officer, writer

Aleksandr Solzhenitsyn, artillery captain, writer

Britons

Brigadier Bolton, commanding officer in Perlin, Mecklenburg

CHAPTER 1

Thunder in the east

What was that? A sound as of distant thunder burst in on the bright summer's day. There it was again, borne by the wind across the sunlit meadows and woods. The horses in the paddocks reared and skittered nervously, nostrils flaring, fear in their large, dark eyes. In the fields and around the stables the farm workers, the apprentices and the uniformed grooms heard it too. Anxiously they tried to judge the distance. Thirty, forty kilometres perhaps, still the other side of the border in Soviet territory, but nevertheless alarmingly close.

They were supposed not to worry. Time and again they had been assured that the Bolsheviks would never gain an inch of German soil. They must trust in the military genius of their great Führer, who would lead them to a glorious victory and seize vast lands for them in the east. The Führer, they were promised, had secret 'wonder weapons' up his sleeve, which he would deploy when he saw fit and annihilate the enemy like magic. They were not even to speak of leaving – that was defeatist. Anyone who prepared to flee was a vile saboteur and could be punished by death.

Most people had long been used to accepting

without question what the authorities told them. Few knew what was really going on. They had trusted Hitler and his henchmen and believed they would never let them come to any harm. And yet … and yet … there were things they were seeing with their own eyes and hearing with their own ears that made them extremely uneasy. As the days passed, the number of those who still believed and still trusted was dwindling rapidly. At home their wives would secretly pack another chest, put aside another ham to sustain them on their journey. 'When are we going?' they would ask, time and again. But the answer, yet again, was silence.

Ernst Ehlert heard the sound too. It confirmed his worst fears. He bore an enormous responsibility and here he was, helpless, forbidden to carry it out. As *Landstallmeister* of Trakehnen, director of the oldest and most prestigious state stud farm in Germany, he was in charge of around 1,200 of the finest horses in the world. Beyond the white-painted Schloss, his official residence and office, grazing in paddocks almost as far as the eye could see, were the products of over two centuries of highly skilled, purposeful breeding: sleek, elegant creatures that combined toughness, speed, intelligence and stamina with astonishing grace and beauty. The Trakehners were a horseman's dream, the perfect cavalry mount, and, to breeders like himself, a gene pool without compare. They were perhaps East Prussia's greatest asset, the core of the breed that was a major source of its fame, income and pride. Yet their lives, and those of more than 3,000 people who cared for them, were being insanely placed in jeopardy.

All through June and now July 1944, the Red Army had been massing just to the east of them, preparing to invade. It was frightening enough that Trakehnen was so close to the border. But recently the Luftwaffe had set up two airfields on the stud's vast grounds, one immediately next to the parade paddock where the horses were shown off to visitors and buyers. Not only was the noise of the machines unnerving the horses, but its presence made the whole area a prime target for Soviet bombers. It stood to reason that the horses and staff must go, and the sooner the better. But those who made such decisions did not respond to reason.

Plans to evacuate Trakehnen in the event of war existed. Ehlert had drawn them up himself, together with local authorities and the agriculture ministry, after he took office in 1931, even though the prospect of war then seemed remote. The horses would be shipped westwards to the presumed safety of the Heilsberg Triangle, the strongly fortified area around the East Prussian capital of Königsberg and its Baltic seaport, Pillau. But these plans were mouldering in some safe in Berlin. Who dared mention them, let alone bring them out? It would be seen as a treasonous lack of confidence in the man who called himself 'the greatest military commander of all time', with consequences that Ehlert would rather not think about. He had asked his superiors in the Food and Agriculture Ministry again and again what preparations were being made for evacuation, but so far had received no reply. All he could do was to make hypothetical arrangements in his head. Anything more than that would be extremely foolish.

Trakehnen was a famous place; many people came and went. Besides, one of his senior officials, Friedrich Kiaulehn, who ran the stud's hunting stables, was the local Nazi Party boss and village mayor. The Gestapo was keeping an ever-tighter watch on the place. And potential informants were everywhere.

Ernst Ehlert was not alone in fearing for the horses in his care. All over East Prussia private breeders – a couple of dozen big landowners and over 10,000 smaller farmers – were afraid not only for their families, themselves and their farms, but also for the fine animals from which they made much of their living. For East Prussia was horse country unlike anywhere else in the world. In this beautiful tract of slightly undulating land between the Baltic Sea in the west and the Lithuanian border to the east, the river Memel in the north to the Polish border in the south, horse breeding and rearing was the major industry. The East Prussians were the main suppliers of mounts to the army; their horses had won innumerable international events all over Europe, including three gold medals and a silver one at the 1936 Olympics, and many thousands were exported each year all over the world. Here, horses were not a status symbol or a hobby for the rich – they were an integral part of everyday life. All of East Prussia's most eminent private breeders had grown up with horses. Hans-Joachim Scharffetter was still a baby when his father Franz first perched him in front of him on the saddle of a full-grown horse. Peter Elxnat was riding bareback before he went to school. After classes Brigitte Pflaumbaum would head straight for the stables to help her father, Emil Pflaumbaum, groom their mares. Few could afford cars or tractors; almost everyone rode or drove horses.

Unlike horse-breeding regions of America or the Soviet Union, there were no prairies or steppes in East Prussia where herds of animals could roam at will, for except for its sandy forests and lakes, the region was cultivated from end to end. Instead the farmers would harness their elegant mares to ploughs or hay carts and work the land, often with foals trotting by their mothers' sides. They owned half as many horses again as farmers in the milder west of Europe, for their winters were much longer and bitterly cold and their growing season six weeks shorter. They needed fast and nimble teams to do all the ploughing, sowing and harvesting in the brief time available. Once a year many would take their mares to be covered by a carefully selected stallion and later sell the foal for a respectable sum, which augmented their income from farming.

While Trakehnen was the core of the breed, the place where it was being constantly improved, refined and adapted to the requirements of the day, it was surrounded by a constellation of private studs where equally superb horses were bred from Trakehnen sires. There were a few huge studs like Weedern, on the banks of the fast-flowing river Angerapp. Weedern belonged to Anna von Zitzewitz, an attractive, witty and dynamic brunette who had been running her own prestigious Trakehner stud at Kleszowen, about 16 kilometres away, when she married Eberhard von Zitzewitz, a highly respected breeder considerably older than herself, who had built up a superb herd of chestnut Trakehners. After his death in 1934, she was left with two young children and the two estates with a total of some 500 horses, which she proceeded to run with characteristic energy.

Further west were the vast estates of the von Kuenheims at Juditten, famous for its brown Trakehners, and those of Prince Alexander zu Dohna at Schlobitten and Prökelwitz, which, as in Trakehnen itself, were divided into herds of different colours. The Dohna stud was run under the skilled eye of the Princess, herself the daughter of an eminent breeder and racehorse owner. A shrewd judge of horses, she had persuaded Ehlert to exchange her superb stallion Polarstern for the young and very promising stallion Indra. Polarstern went on to become one of Trakehnen's most famous sires, while Indra gave the Dohnas a long succession of superb sons and daughters. Although it was becoming old-fashioned, the Princess loved riding side-saddle, an art she had been taught in her youth by a head groom of the Imperial Mews in Berlin.

Numerous breeders were descendants of the Protestants from Salzburg, brought in a couple of centuries earlier to populate the land. One such man was Franz Scharffetter, the son of the late Johann Scharffetter, a man whose enormous bulk, walrus moustache and eccentric nature were as famous throughout the province as his liking for East Prussia's favourite tipple, which had earned him the nickname 'King of Grog'. Johann had taken over the badly run-down estate of Kallwischken, near Insterburg, in 1895 and built it up into one of the best private studs in East Prussia. When he retired he handed it over to his son Franz, who went on to win many top prizes for his mares and produced stallions that became Trakehnen sires. Franz, although slimmer than his father, was likewise a character, given to escapades and pranks, one of which involved appearing on horseback to guests sleeping in the attic of his farm. How he got the horse up to the attic, history does not relate. Franz was not averse to grog himself and during one night's drinking had rashly compared the Führer to Frederick the Great in highly uncomplimentary terms. It was only his popularity among the locals that saved him from denunciation and a very nasty fate.

Some breeders could trace their ancestry back to the early knight-settlers. Among these was Johanna Haedge-Medicus, a tall, raven-haired woman whose family owned large estates near the Polish border, where Polish was spoken almost as much as German. The large estate of Sabloczyn, only 3 kilometres from the border, belonged to a wealthy bachelor uncle without heirs and was therefore in imminent danger of being confiscated by the Nazis, broken up and distributed to small farmers. It was being managed by Karl Sasse, a former cavalry captain and also a bachelor. Although he was old enough to be her father, Johanna married him, they had two children and the estate remained in the family.

However, most of East Prussia's Trakehners were bred on much smaller farms by small-time farmers who proudly owned about two brood mares each, yet still produced horses of extremely high quality. The bigger estate owners were remnants of an archaic society that was dying out in much of the rest of Europe. Many were nobility, although few had titles and some had dropped the aristocratic prefix 'von' from their surnames. A few were wealthy but many were deeply indebted, as their fathers and grandfathers had been for decades. Some were highly educated, well travelled and liberal minded, but on the whole they tended to be extremely conservative. Under the Kaisers and during the ill-fated Weimar Republic they had wielded considerable political power and made themselves unpopular with many other Germans; but now their situation was different. Some were enthusiastic Nazis, but many were unimpressed or alienated by their behaviour and bizarre new ideas.

These East Prussian families had a long and proud military tradition; for generations they had staffed the Prussian army and East Prussian officers still held prominent positions in Hitler's Wehrmacht. At home some of these landowners could be arrogant and coarse, and were somewhat unfairly considered by outsiders to be typical of their caste. They were known as Junkers, a name which – like that of Prussia itself – was for many years to bear negative overtones which in fact masked a much more varied society.

On their farms and estates these landowners were usually extremely hard working. They still employed many staff whose families had lived and worked on their estates for generations and who they often paid partly in kind: firewood, provisions, plots of land and livestock. But it was more than just a working relationship: the estate owners had not only privileges but also duties and responsibilities towards their people, and they were about to face these responsibilities again in a way that had seldom happened before.

The East Prussian Studbook Society, which represented the private breeders, had made careful and detailed arrangements for evacuation. Foals and young horses in particular were to be shipped out by train and placed in the care of other breeders' associations in Mecklenburg, Pomerania and further west. But as Anna von Zitzewitz found when she sent large numbers of her horses to safety on her brother-in-law's estate at Gross-Gansen in Pomerania and elsewhere, to do so was to incur massive hostility and harassment from the Nazi Party and the party-controlled farmers' organisations. Many owners were not able to send out their horses at all.

PEOPLE AND HORSES had lived and worked together in this part of the world for well over a thousand years. Back in the Dark Ages the local tribe, the Pruzzen, rode and probably drove horses and could send thousands of mounted warriors into battle. In the 13th century, when the first Crusader knights of the Teutonic Order arrived on the scene, summoned by a Polish ruler to subdue and Christianise the troublesome Pruzzen, they brought with them their heavy warhorses. They set up over 60 studs to reproduce these horses, muscular beasts that could bear the weight of a man in full armour, travel long distances and behave fearlessly in battle. As the knights settled and became farmers, and brought in relatives and friends from other parts of Germany to help populate the land, their helpmates in the fields were not the big warhorses but the horses the Pruzzen kept, mousy little creatures called *Schweike*. Close relatives of the wild horses that still roamed the forests and steppes of central and eastern Europe, they were tough, strong and undemanding and able to work hard for long hours on little fodder. They rarely fell ill and were extremely cheap to keep. For 400 years most ordinary farmers seemed content to work and breed or cross-breed their *Schweike*, until the 18th century brought a dramatic change.

When Ernst Ehlert surveyed Trakehnen's carefully manicured parks, the immaculately kept red-brick stables, the well-swept paths, neat houses and vast, lush meadows, it would have been hard to imagine what it had been like 200 years previously. For the whole area had been covered by swamps, reeds and rushes, willows and alders. The only sounds would have been from the storks, clattering their bills over their nests, the wild boar grunting through the undergrowth, or the occasional roar of an elk. Here and there might have been the odd ruined homestead, burned down in one of many wars or deserted by its owners, starving after a series of failed harvests or killed off by the plague. Trakehnen (*Trakis* meant 'burnt-out forest' in the language of early Lithuanian settlers who gave many places here their names) was a desolate, empty wasteland. But then came soldiers, 600 of them, who set to work draining the swamps. They created fertile, arable land and built a huge stud farm designed by none less than the king himself. When all was finished, six years later, the 1,101 royal horses, originally scattered in various mews and studs all over Prussia, were assembled here and in 1732 the Royal Trakehnen Stud Farm opened for business.

Trakehnen had been part of a campaign by King Friedrich Wilhelm I to repopulate the area and make it prosper. Around that time, with his policy of religious tolerance, he had attracted to Prussia some 130,000 refugees from various types of religious persecution: Huguenots, Swiss Protestants, Mennonites, Jews or Catholics, as well as Polish, Scottish, English and Dutch immigrants. In particular he brought in some 21,000 Salzburg Protestants and settled most of them, at vast expense, around Trakehnen. Even his son, Crown Prince Friedrich (later known to the English-speaking world as Frederick the Great), who had little love for his tyrannical father, admitted in a letter to his mentor Voltaire that there was 'something heroic in the generous and zealous way in which the King has colonised this desert and made it fertile.'

King Friedrich Wilhelm wanted Trakehnen to produce a steady supply of riding and carriage horses for himself and his court. And at the same time he hoped that by selling off the surplus it would make a handsome profit for the royal coffers. In this last matter he was disappointed. The economics had been badly thought out: Trakehnen did not produce enough fodder for all its horses, and the staff, wretchedly underpaid and demoralised, responded by cheating and stealing. Seven years later Friedrich Wilhelm gave the stud to his son, who showed little interest in it. He saw Trakehnen mainly as a cash-cow, failed to invest in it, yet repeatedly threatened to close it down unless his profits doubled. The horses were a motley collection from many countries and breeds and many were of indifferent quality. The idea of serious, scientific breeding had not yet taken root – it was the fashion in those days to try and cross the most diverse animals. Even Trakehnen was to be instructed at one point to mate horses and donkeys with bulls and cows in the hopes of producing an animal that had the advantages of all. Nevertheless the director of the day, Johann Friedrich von Domhardt, did the best he could under difficult circumstances. He brought in English and Arab horses to improve the stock and the first results were encouraging. Friedrich took undeserved pride in the fact that Trakehner carriage horses beat the best English horses over the distance from his palace of Sanssouci in Potsdam to Berlin, with half an hour to spare.

This was at a time when Friedrich was turning Prussia into an ambitious new European power. He had a huge and formidable army, raised to conquer other lands in order to unite and expand the scattered possessions that his family had acquired by chance and inheritance. This army needed good horses, most of which he had to buy abroad, which was both costly and fraught with risks. Some of them had to come from as far away as Bessarabia and the Crimea: horses whose journey, on foot, often took a good year and when they arrived – if they arrived at all, and around one-fifth didn't – were pitifully weak and emaciated. Friedrich realised that Prussia needed to be self-sufficient in mounts. But his efforts to rely on the domestic supply failed: neither Trakehnen nor Prussian farmers could produce enough suitable horses, most being still too small for the army's requirements. Later von Domhardt proposed a plan to the King under which he could save a large part of the fortune that he spent on foreign horses by mating Trakehner stallions with Prussian farmers' mares. But by then Friedrich felt too old and weary to embark on a new project and the plan was shelved.

However, Friedrich's nephew and successor, Friedrich Wilhelm II, needed no persuading. Only a few weeks after ascending the throne he gave orders for large sums of money to be invested in stallion depots around the country. There every spring farmers' working mares were to be covered, free of charge, by Trakehnen's best sires. These depots developed over the years into *Landgestüte*, regional state stud farms, which housed the stallions when they were not out on mating duty. The *Hauptgestüt*, or main state stud farm at Trakehnen, remained the place where the best sires and brood mares were kept to develop and perfect the breed, to filter out undesirable characteristics and produce further generations of top-quality sires to serve the horse population of the region. Thus the state funds that previously went to foreign horse dealers were diverted to Prussian farmers and the remarkable partnership between Prussia's military and its agriculture was sealed. And so began the state's involvement in horse breeding: a model that was repeated in other German states and in France, while in England and Ireland it was left entirely to private enterprise.

The turning point for Trakehnen and the basis of its future glory was a decision by Friedrich Wilhelm II to appoint Carl Heinrich August, Count von Lindenau, as his *Oberlandstallmeister*, or Master of Horse, to provide him with adequate funds and instruct him to reorganise the breeding system. Von Lindenau weeded out the many weak and defective horses in Trakehnen – nearly half the stock – selling them off and bringing in new blood. He allowed only good-quality farmers' mares, which received an appropriate brand, to be covered by the state stallions and issued strict rules to limit unauthorised breeding. Each foal sired by a Trakehner stallion had to be presented to the stud authorities at the age of two. The males that were considered suitable for breeding were bought for a set sum and the owner was presented with a gold medal worth 40 Talers. The rest were castrated and sold as high-quality riding or carriage horses or cavalry mounts.

Count von Lindenau decreed that from then he would use 'only pure gold' as far as stallions were concerned. He invested heavily in English horses for their height and large frames. For until then Trakehnen mares had been worryingly small, only five feet at the withers, probably due to the influence of the *Schweike*.

The second most important influence on the Trakehner lineage was Arab and Anglo-Arab stallions. Bred and hardened for over a thousand years in the severe desert climate of their homelands, Arab horses brought a special toughness, hardiness and stamina into the breed, along with natural good health and a good-natured temperament. They also tended to be highly fertile, long-lived and able to recover quickly after great stress. They also gave Trakehners much of their beauty: large eyes, well-balanced proportions and graceful movements. Thus English and Arab blood, combined with the frugality, toughness and sturdiness inherited from the *Schweike*, were the building blocks of the breed. This mix was to be used for generations, albeit with variations according to the requirements of the day. It produced horses of remarkable strength and stamina. The temperatures in East Prussia ranged from some 30 degrees centigrade in summer to minus 30 degrees in winter, but the Trakehners could live outside if necessary and never needed blankets.

From 1787 Trakehners were distinguishable not only by their physical beauty, but also by the brand on their right rump: a single antler of an elk, the huge creature that roamed the East Prussian forests. Later, from 1888 onwards, the certified descendants of Trakehner stallions, those bred from Trakehner sires and private breeders' mares, and registered in the East Prussian studbook, received a double elk's antler on the left rump. Officially these were called East Prussian Warmblood horses of Trakehner Descent.

One of the greatest milestones in the breeding of Trakehners was in 1903, when the Prussian government's Master of Horse, Georg Count von Lehndorff, and the *Landstallmeister* of Trakehnen, Burchard von Oettingen (both familiar figures in top international breeding circles), went to England and bought the English thoroughbred, Perfectionist. Perfectionist was the son of Persimmon, the famous stallion owned by King Edward VII, which in 1896 had won the two greatest races, the Derby and the St Leger. Persimmon, in turn, was the son of the legendary St Simon, a stallion so fast that he won all the races he ever entered without even extending himself. St

Simon once caused a sensation by winning the two-and-a-half-mile Ascot Gold Cup by 20 lengths, and then tearing on for another mile before he finally consented to stop. Perfectionist, who was dark brown, only stood for three years in Trakehnen before this superb and extremely expensive stallion had to be destroyed after breaking his pelvis in a tragic fall in his loose box.

Perfectionist was one of many English thoroughbreds to be used in Trakehnen, but his was a very special legacy: 131 foals, of which 32 stallions and 37 mares were of such superb quality that they were reserved for breeding and it was they who determined to a great extent the Trakehner of the 20th century. Perfectionist's greatest son was the legendary Tempelhüter, also dark brown, who in turn produced many important sires and whose statue stood in front of the Schloss at Trakehnen. With Perfectionist's descendants, and other valuable sires such as Dampfross, Ernst Ehlert was credited with having brought the quality of Trakehnen's horses up to the highest standard yet achieved. The Trakehner was a beautiful animal, with a small, lean head and large, wide-set eyes, alert ears, a long graceful neck, sloping shoulders, lean, sinewy legs, light-footed and supple. It was also good-natured and willing; any with signs of bad temper or viciousness was immediately weeded out from the stud.

WAS EVERYTHING that Ehlert and his predecessors had built up to be annihilated?

Prussia had repeatedly been ravaged by wars during its history and this was not the first time Trakehnen had been in danger. Four times the stud's staff and horses had had to flee. In 1794 they were moved westwards as unrest in Poland threatened to spill over the border. Twice during the Napoleonic Wars they had to go, fleeing in 1806 into – then – friendly, Russian-controlled Lithuania and in 1812 into Silesia. During the Napoleonic Wars a total of some 180,000 horses perished in East Prussia, a terrible loss for breeders and farmers.

But that had been more than a century ago. What had burned itself deepest into Trakehnen inhabitants' minds was the First World War, when they had fled westwards in terror from the Russians, and returned after the invaders had been driven out, to find many of their homes and the stud buildings devastated. Only in 1919 had enough buildings been rebuilt or repaired for all Trakehnen's horses to return. In that war around 135,000 East Prussian horses perished – more than half the entire stock of the province, including 25,000 brood mares. Older people remembered those days vividly and spoke of them often, imparting advice to their children and grandchildren on how to prepare for flight and pressing them to get going soon.

If only they *could* flee again. But this time it was different. First one madman here in Germany, and then another in Moscow, with many willing supporters, had turned war into a savage and barbarous orgy of cruelty, enslavement and annihilation. Whether they had believed in Hitler or not, they were helpless pawns in deranged schemes in which their lives, welfare and property were of no importance whatever.

There was still no reply from Berlin. If Ehlert were to

save Trakehnen's horses and people, he would have to be persistent, circumspect, inventive and cunning – and take immense risks.

CHAPTER 2

A Nazi thug takes over

The Ehlerts' granddaughter, Lilli Grundmann, came to Trakehnen aged 10 in 1939 with her mother and four-year-old brother. Her father, a lawyer in their hometown of Treptow in Pomerania, had just been called up into the army and her mother wanted to be with her own parents. It turned out to be a good decision, because there they were safe from the Allied bombs that were to devastate many German cities and claim countless lives. East Prussia, which lay beyond the range of the bombers, would remain for several years far from the war, a haven of tranquillity.

Lilli went to one of the nine elementary schools for Trakehnen children and later joined some 20 other older ones who went by train to secondary school in the nearby town of Gumbinnen. Each day the children would gather by an old oak tree at seven in the morning to be collected and driven the 6 kilometres to Trakehnen station in a horse-drawn carriage: in the summer an open wagon, in the bitterly cold winters a covered conveyance with thick straw on the floor to provide a minimum of warmth. Since increasing numbers of Trakehnen's men were being drafted into the army, the children were often driven by Helmut Hufenbach, an apprentice groom not much older than they, and fetched by him again in the afternoon when they returned. For Lilli and many others in East Prussia, the war seemed a little remote and unreal, something one heard about on the radio and read about, in bombastic terms, in the dwindling supply of newspapers. Men would don uniforms and go off to the front, and black military crosses would multiply in the deaths columns of the newspapers. There were troop movements; neighbouring Poland had been invaded and swiftly conquered despite heroic resistance, of which they learned little. There were some shortages, but much less so than in the rest of Germany. In the country, especially in Trakehnen, which was self-sufficient in most things, life went on almost as normal, far from the horrors of war. Most East Prussians knew only what little the Party-controlled media were allowed to tell them. Listening to foreign radio stations was severely punished. Not many people – only those with knowledge of the world outside, those who knew what was really going on and could think ahead – were able to foresee the cataclysm inexorably bearing down on them.

Yet there had been signs, for those who could interpret them. Roads that led eastwards, towards the Lithuanian-Soviet border, were being asphalted. Lookout towers were being built close to the border. Loaded lorries were being driven past the estate of Lenken and into the dark pine forest through which the frontier ran. The local Nazis put it about that they were loads of turnips, to feed the game because the forest was going to be turned into a hunting range for Reichsmarschall Hermann Göring and other Nazi bosses. The von Sperbers soon guessed that the 'turnips' were munitions destined to be used against Russia. General (later Field Marshal) Erich von Manstein, who led the LVI (56th) Panzerkorps, was billeted with his staff in Lenken. When they tackled him about the 'turnips' he laughed, but did not try to deny that they were munitions. Then he remarked, in words they would long remember, 'it would be the height of madness to attack Russia'.

Rastenburg, some 70 kilometres from Trakehnen, was a small town with a castle built by the Teutonic Knights and a *Landgestüt* with some 140 stallions that served the area. About four miles to the east there was a thick forest where Rastenburgers would go for walks, hold open-air parties in summer or dance in the *Kursaal* of a local village. But in the autumn of 1940 much of the forest had been cordoned off. Gangs of workmen moved in and started clearing trees, digging trenches, laying roads and gardens, building barracks, blockhouses and finally huge bunkers with walls several yards thick, all supposedly a new plant for the Askania chemical works. An airfield was laid out close by, the local railway line was closed to civilian traffic and a huge, crack SS guard moved into barracks inside and outside the town. The area was surrounded by a 10-foot-wide barbed-wire entanglement, minefields and an anti-tank ditch. It was being constantly extended, while green camouflage netting overhead and anti-aircraft batteries protected it from detection or attack from the air. Long before the arrival of Hitler in 1941, with his top military and party leaders, it had become clear that this was no chemical works. It was the *Wolfsschanze*: the Wolf's Lair, the fortress from which Hitler was to direct Operation Barbarossa, the invasion and annihilation of the Soviet Union and the destruction of Communism.

As Hitler and his generals pored over their maps, Barbara von Sperber had other things on her mind. A pretty, blonde aristocrat from Saxony with the domestic science diploma fashionable among young girls of good family background, she was 23 when she found herself mistress of the large and prestigious Lenken estate, in 1936. Her father-in-law, Hans-Erhard von Sperber, had been killed in a tragic accident in his horse-drawn carriage only shortly before her wedding and she and her husband, a dashing cavalry officer, had moved into the big house and taken charge of the Lenken stud, as well as its pedigree cattle and pigs. Now with her husband away with his mounted regiment, first in Poland, then in France, and her family rapidly increasing, she was in sole command. It was not easy for her here in the furthest reaches of East Prussia. She was an outsider, she spoke with the distinctive Saxon accent that other Germans found comical, and although she loved animals, she knew nothing about breeding horses. She had the advice and help of Martin Heling, at the Georgenburg *Landgestüt*, and of her husband when he came home on leave. But as one relative was to remark later, she had a natural talent, and soon became a good breeder in her own right. As her staff were increasingly drafted into the armed forces, she found a valuable assistant in a former class-mate from her boarding school who had experience with horses.

Lenken Trakehners were legendary for their nobility,

grace and light, effortless movement. After the First World War, when the trend in breeding was towards stronger, heavier horses, her father-in-law had preferred to continue producing the classical, light Trakehner type. The huge estate between the rivers Memel and Szeszuppe was ideal breeding land with its light, sandy soil and great rolling meadows.

The main customer for generations of von Sperbers, Zitzewitzes and other East Prussian breeders had been been the armed forces. Private buyers had come second. But after the First World War, under the harsh terms of the Versailles treaty imposed on Germany by the victorious Allies, the situation was reversed. Germany was allowed an army of only 100,000 men. The cavalry was cut from 100 regiments to 18 and the breeders were forced desperately to seek new markets. They had to mount publicity and marketing campaigns to sell their horses for riding, show jumping and dressage purposes. They held auctions in other parts of the German Reich, organised hunts, steeplechases, exhibitions, markets and other equestrian events in an effort to attract customers – and attract them they did. They exported thousands of horses to countries all over the world.

But it was not enough. They still had to sell off many horses at half or even a third of what it had cost to breed and raise them. Of these, 5,000 went to the Soviet Union, where they continued to be bred on state farms, mostly in the traditional horse-breeding area around Rostov-on-the-Don and crossed with English thoroughbreds to produce racing horses. Trakehnen itself had to cut down the number of its horses and staff, and for some years its financial basis was alarmingly precarious. Under its then *Landstallmeister* or director, Siegfried Count von Lehndorff, and later under Dr Ehlert, Trakehnen had to develop a bigger, longer and stronger horse which was more suitable for agriculture than the lighter cavalry mounts that it had produced before. They achieved this brilliantly, using the heavier stallions and mares within the breed and without needing to bring in new blood from other, bigger breeds.

In 1934 Hitler started building up the German armed forces in secret. The following year he publicly repudiated the Versailles treaty of 1919, and rapidly built the armed forces up again, initially to around half a million men. By this time Prussia had long since ceased to be an independent state and was now just another region – albeit by far the largest and most influential – within the Reich. With the new military build-up, the breeders' prospects were to change again. But meanwhile a long and fierce debate had been raging in the German military, as in the armies of other countries, about the future of horses in increasingly mechanised forces. Those who – correctly – saw the future of war in tanks and armoured vehicles, dismissed horses as useless; the cavalry considered them indispensable. Experience soon showed that the cavalry were right, but not in the way they imagined. About nine out of ten German divisions in the east were still unmechanised. Horses were needed to transport artillery and equipment. The Wehrmacht's demand for horses rose vertiginously: by 1939 it had over 170,000, which already made it the biggest animal-owner in the country and this figure was to rise to more than a million over the next five years. Once again, business for breeders was flourishing and prices of horses were soaring so high that the government had to step in to control them.

The most important day of the year for Barbara von Sperber was the Lenken mount sales, usually held in May. This was when the army's purchasing commission would come to Lenken to buy three-year-olds to be trained for military use. Mount markets were usually held in public, but some were also held in the estate yards of large private breeders.

The family's finances depended to a great extent on the number of three-year-olds they were able to sell and for days or weeks beforehand they would rehearse with their young animals, teaching them to stand still and go through their paces so they would be seen to the best advantage. They would be brushed and burnished till they shone, their hooves thoroughly manicured, their manes carefully plaited and their long tails combed. The horses were tied up around the courtyard, alongside those of other breeders from the vicinity. The uniformed commission was led by a *Remontepräsis*, a cavalry officer, who often bore an aristocratic title. This was no snobbery: the army needed officers with a thorough knowledge of horses and of the army's needs. Few could offer this better than a Prussian aristocrat or landowner with a long family tradition of service in the cavalry and often of horse breeding at home. One may have been Karl Sasse, who, as war broke out, had been drafted back into the army. He would be accompanied by two or three other officers, also experts: one with a measuring-stick, another with the cash box and a couple of soldiers to handle the horses.

One by one the horses would be led out, and each one put through its paces. Then a groom or a soldier would stand squarely facing the horse's head, holding the reins at each side of the bit to keep the animal still. The horse would be measured, carefully inspected, and if it was promising, put on a shortlist of horses that were later again made to walk and trot in a circle past the commission. When they had seen them all, the commission went into a huddle and finally someone read out the numbers of the horses that would be bought. There were sighs of relief, or groans of despair from the owners, for rejected horses were likely to bring a much lower price elsewhere.

That evening the breeder would traditionally give a splendid dinner for the commission and other guests, hopefully to celebrate their success in selling large numbers of horses. The story was told of one breeder who had planned to have caviar served at dinner. However, when the market went badly and many of his horses were rejected, he ran into the kitchens and shouted to the cook: 'No caviar tonight!'

Meanwhile the soldiers would be loading the horses that had been chosen into trucks and driving them away. For Barbara the sight of her horses leaving was a bittersweet moment. Each sale was important, but she was always heartbroken to watch the tender young animals that they had so lovingly raised going off with the soldiers to an unknown fate.

But for the time being their horses would be, almost

literally, in clover. They were taken to a military depot where for a year they and many others were put out to graze and fed special fodder to ensure that all were in top condition for the moment when they would be distributed to the various regiments. Some of the best riding horses were sent not far away to Insterburg, where her husband's 1st Prussian Mounted Regiment and a Horse Artillery Battalion were based. There, a stocky, round-faced cavalryman called Peter Elxnat and other experienced horsemen would ride them in, gently during the first year and more intensively the second, until they were ready to join the troops.

Elxnat was the latest in one of East Prussia's oldest families of smaller Trakehner breeders. They produced excellent quality animals on their two farms and Peter had lived among horses since he was born. At the age of 18, with military service looming, he volunteered for the cavalry and, because of his background, was accepted. Others were not so lucky; there were far more volunteers for the cavalry than places available and his company could pick the best. Potential officers in particular flocked to the mounted regiments because they wanted to learn to ride – much to the annoyance of General Heinz Guderian, later army chief of staff, who was working to organise Germany's new panzer forces. 'Why don't they learn to be mechanics?' he grumbled.

It was not only the horse-breeders who had suffered in the wake of the First World War. East Prussia as a whole had been dealt a severe economic and psychological blow by the Versailles treaty. It had been cut off geographically from western Prussia and the rest of Germany in order to give Poland, newly restored as an independent state after 23 years of obliteration, its 'corridor', a swathe of land that gave it access to the sea. Farmers were in desperate straits all over the Germany, but in rural East Prussia, with its outdated agricultural system, the situation was often critical. The radical *Bauernnotbewegung* – Farmers' Emergency Movement – a protest movement that was given to physically resisting the expropriation of bankrupt farms, found fertile ground in East Prussia, where one of its leaders was the gifted speaker and landowner, Max Haedge-Medicus. The Nazi Party, too, had been busily fishing in these turbulent and fertile waters.

The real and perceived difficulties, combined with inflation, had devastating political results. East Prussia had been a deeply conservative province: in the 1928 elections the right-wing German National Party had won the biggest share of the vote, 31.4 per cent, while Hitler's new National Socialist, or Nazi, Party, had only 0.8 per cent, the lowest of any state in the Reich. But in the last, still reasonably democratic, elections in 1933 the Nazis rocketed to 56.5 per cent, the highest figure for anywhere in Germany except Pomerania. When Hitler seized power shortly afterwards, the fate of millions of people was sealed: the Nazi official, Erich Koch, was made Gauleiter of East Prussia – effectively governor of the whole region.

Of all Hitler's unsavoury Gauleiters, Koch was by far one of the most repulsive. A short, stocky railway clerk from Elberfeld, near Wuppertal, with a turbulent past, he had no professional qualifications but immense cunning, criminal energy and an insatiable thirst for power and possessions. These he knew he could get by a fanatical pursuit of Hitler's aims and espousal of his ideas; he even affected the Führer's toothbrush moustache. He was a demagogue, an adventurer and not without talents, particularly when it came to pleasing Hitler. But he was also savage, brutal, lawless and shamelessly corrupt, and once in power in East Prussia he swept out leading politicians and functionaries and put his own henchmen in key positions. Just as Hitler surrounded himself with people fanatically devoted to him and ready to do his bidding, Koch totally controlled East Prussia with a network of party officials, particularly district and village bosses, all over the province who obeyed him blindly. He even held the SS at arm's length for fear they might undermine his own power – which did not mean, however, that Jews and political opponents were treated any less savagely than elsewhere.

Many of his men were thugs and convicted criminals; one was even mentally handicapped. East Prussians who retained the old Prussian ethos of rectitude in public office were scandalised, but those who opposed him were mercilessly eliminated, or thrown out of their jobs without pension. 'Anyone who bites me dies from it', he is reputed to have said. He was also quoted as saying: 'Money is lying everywhere on the street, one only has to bend down and pick it up.' And he bent down many times. When he took office he announced that to set an example he would not live in the president's official residence but in a modest four-room apartment that would also serve as his office. Simultaneously he was planning to move into the Königsberg Schloss, and only changed his mind when persuaded that this would give a bad impression. He then obliged the city to buy him a large and beautiful suburban villa, which had belonged to Jews. Soon dissatisfied with that, he demanded and obtained a large estate called Gross Friedrichsberg outside the city, and spent many millions of Reichsmarks from public coffers expanding it and installing himself in unheard-of luxury. Even the cowsheds and stables were centrally heated. His lavish lifestyle soon earned him the nickname of 'Duke Erich'. Extremely cynical and fully aware that he, like many others before him, one day may fall foul of Hitler, he was believed to have had his wife take out much of his ill-gotten money to safety in Argentina and also to buy them a farm there as a bolthole. At times when things became too hot for him, he would have a plane waiting with its engine running at the local airport, ready to take off at a moment's notice.

He launched the East Prussia Plan, later known as the Erich Koch Plan, for the economic reform of the province. This included schemes for the industrialisation of the region and for collectivisation of agriculture, which made him extremely unpopular with the farmers. Koch took over the leadership of the party's farmers' organisations and banned the *Bauernnotbewegung*. He declared at a public meeting that its leader, 'that old reactionary, Haedge-Medicus, should be smeared with tar and burned in the market place'. Beside himself with rage and without thought for the consequences, Haedge-Medicus challenged Koch to a duel with pistols. Duelling, of course, was outlawed, but in any case

Haedge-Medicus had practically signed his own death warrant: such rebellion automatically led to Roland Freisler's notorious *Volksgerichtshof* (People's Court) in Berlin, and from there to the gallows. But fortunately Haedge-Medicus had been a First World War flying ace, along with Hermann Göring, Air Minister and one of Hitler's most powerful henchmen. Göring detested Koch, whom he dismissed as a 'ticket-clipper'. He promptly drafted Haedge-Medicus into the Luftwaffe and forced Koch to sign a formal declaration exonerating him of any wrongdoing. Haedge-Medicus's life was saved.

Koch's Plan achieved little. It gave birth, however, to the Erich Koch Foundation, which served as a front for him to gain personal possession of some 150 industries. He extorted money from Jews, before having them stripped of their belongings and sent to extermination camps. He appropriated both public and charitable funds destined to alleviate hardship among East Prussians. Within a few years of taking office, Koch had turned much of the population against him and his nickname changed to 'the brown Tsar of East Prussia' – brown being the Nazi Party colour. He was loathed not only by Göring, but also by Hitler's powerful propaganda minister, Joseph Goebbels, and the SS chief, Heinrich Himmler, and he even horrified the SS itself. George Ebrecht, a senior SS officer and chief of police in Königsberg, was to write three years later, somewhat cautiously, in a letter to the national police chief Richard Hildebrandt: 'Koch is a brilliant rascal.' Germany needed people, he went on, who at least knew good from bad, right from wrong. 'His undoubted abilities do nothing but harm. All sense of legality is completely overturned.' On the subject of Koch, Hildebrandt had no such inhibitions. He replied to Ebrecht: 'A man like Koch should be hanged from the highest tree ... I don't even think he is brilliant. He is a man who conducts politics with gangster methods.'

Curiously, however, Koch appeared to have a genuine religious streak in him. Brought up a Protestant, and once an assiduous participant in Bible-reading sessions of the Young Men's Christian Association, he protected the East Prussian Evangelical church – on condition, of course, that it remained loyal to the regime. He even, alone among Gauleiters, held high posts in the church, although he clearly did not believe that its precepts applied to himself.

East Prussians had long been trying behind the scenes to have Koch removed. One of these was Alexander zu Dohna-Schlobitten, one of the province's biggest landowners. In 1934 he had invited Göring to a hunting weekend on his estates in the company of prominent East Prussian figures who, like himself, were strongly opposed to Koch. Göring was a powerful figure in East Prussia. Among his many offices he was Prime Minister of Prussia – later he became its Interior Minister, which gave him great powers over the police and civil service – and he was frequently involved in East Prussian affairs. Moreover, as a First World War hero and (unlike most top Nazis) able to move easily and affably in society, he inspired more confidence among the East Prussian upper class than the others. The weekend passed, Göring slept in the room where the Kaiser had once stayed, listened to what his host and fellow guests had to say, ate a lot, shot three stags and went away well pleased. But Koch remained in his job.

A year later it looked as if they might have had some influence after all. A courageous Königsberg city councillor, Paul Wolff, had denounced Koch for a long list of crimes and misdemeanours in a memorandum sent to Hitler personally. At the urging, it was believed, of Göring and Himmler, Hitler ordered formal investigations to be conducted by a committee headed by Himmler. During the investigations, a group of Koch's opponents secretly mounted a watch on his plane, which was waiting at the airfield, determined to shoot him if he tried to escape. Instead, Koch was found guilty, arrested and taken off to be shot. But a month later he was miraculously back in office again, supported by official announcements that the allegations were all untrue and Hitler had the greatest confidence in him. Why? Hitler had long considered Koch his best Gauleiter, but this may not be the reason he spared him. In East Prussia it was rumoured, and widely believed, that Koch had threatened that if he was harmed, highly damaging material he had collected and hidden abroad about Hitler and other Nazi bosses would be published. Not for the last time, he had narrowly succeeded in saving his own skin.

When Koch returned to Königsberg, Göring was forced to make an hour-and-a-half-long speech to all the top officials and Nazi leaders of East Prussia praising him and dismissing all accusations against him. Afterwards Göring was ceremonially presented with the honorary citizenship of the city. But when he and Koch emerged on the town hall steps expecting to be cheered by the crowd, the reception they got was icy. Not a single person raised their arm in the *Heil Hitler* salute. The crowd remained completely silent.

Back at his desk, Koch, who had already personally hit Wolff in the face with his fist in fury at his memorandum, promptly ordered his assassination. It turned out to be an absurdly bungled attempt, which Wolff easily spotted and foiled, but he continued to be persecuted for years.

As the 1932 elections showed, many East Prussians, like other Germans, had seen Hitler and his party as their great hope for an end to the economic problems and political turbulence of the time. Many joined the Nazi Party, some out of conviction, others in the hopes of a career, others simply to hang on to their jobs. Dr Ehlert had been appointed to his post before the Nazis took power and only attempted to join the Party, possibly as a precaution. four years after it came to power. But his application was rejected by the district Party leadership, for reasons unknown. There are indications, however, that he may have been accepted later on.

With the Nazis in power, politics and government had become a treacherous business and not even horsebreeding was safe from its intrigues. On the warm recommendation of a friend from his student days, the new Agriculture Minister, Richard Walther Darré, appointed the world-famous, immensely influential horse expert, Gustav Rau, as Prussian *Oberlandstallmeister* in charge of state horsebreeding and other equestrian matters. But some Nazi bosses wanted the job for themselves, while others were just out to ruin him. Rau was accused of embezzling large amounts of state money, but three separate investigations, by the Attorney General, the Ministry and the Party, all cleared him. What he did not survive was his fight to prevent Germany's many equestrian associations, the *Zucht- Reit- und Fahrvereine*, to which huge numbers of horsepeople belonged, from being absorbed into the SA and SS. If they had to lose their independence, he wanted them to be attached to the less politicised Wehrmacht. He was forced to resign.

Darré then asked a university friend, Dr Hans Seyffert, first to stand in for Rau and then to take over the job himself. Darré was a Nazi ideologue, the father of the party's racist, back-to-the-land 'Blood and Soil' programme, but he was also one of the few Nazi ministers who actually was an expert in his field. Seyffert, balding and slightly baby-faced, was. although by no means the best candidate, at least qualified for the job: he had a degree in agriculture and had been *Landstallmeister* first at the Marienwerder stud in East Prussia and then at Leubus in Silesia. Both state and private breeders, who had pressured him hard to take the job and prevent some incompetent Nazi getting it, breathed sighs of relief when he reluctantly agreed.

But that was not the end of the story. Darré was also the head of the SS's *Rasse und Siedlungshauptamt* (*RuSHA*), or Race and Settlement Office, an outfit which at the time screened potential members of the SS and their future wives for racial 'purity'. And in 1936 Seyffert was made an honorary member of the *RuSHA* staff, probably acting as a consultant on genetic matters. He had joined the SS the previous year, was rapidly working his way up its ranks and probably went around in its smart black uniform. But he was also a horseman, and as he navigated the dangerous waters in Berlin, he was without doubt on the side of the breeders and their horses.

What could happen to those who did not cosy up to the new regime was painfully demonstrated by Ehlert's colleague Martin Heling, who, although uninterested in politics, instinctively disliked the Nazis, their ideas and methods, and did not even try to join. He was an extremely capable breeder and administrator and was seen as a possible future head of Trakehnen; in 1930 he was appointed *Landstallmeister* of the large and highly prestigious 18th-century state stud farm at Neustadt on the river Dosse, northwest of Berlin. Only two weeks after the 1933 elections he was asked at a party what he thought of that day's speech by Göring on the radio. Trying cautiously to avoid giving an opinion, he said the reception on his radio set was so bad that it sounded as if the speaker was drunk. Heling's assistant, presumably a Nazi, promptly denounced him, alleging that he had said Göring was drunk. The man added in his denunciation: 'Our farmers will beat this swine to death, he should be taken into protective custody.'

Heling was suspended pending investigations, but was later reinstated and the assistant fired. But from then on he suffered intense and nerve-racking harassment by the Party, which climaxed in 1933 with his transfer to the smaller and much less important state stud farm at Rastenburg. It was a humiliation clearly designed to induce him to resign. Wisely, he gritted his teeth and stuck it out. His fortitude was rewarded in 1937, when Seyffert appointed him to Georgenburg, the biggest and most prestigious of East Prussian state stud farms, in a move that was seen by all as his rehabilitation.

CHAPTER 3

A horses' paradise

Lilli was unaware of all these things as she stayed with her grandparents at Trakehnen, for those were times when children were told little or nothing about politics or the harsher things of life. Trakehnen and its daily life were all-absorbing.

Lilli and her grandparents lived in the simple but charming white-painted Schloss, a gracious manor house with climbing plants trained up the walls and topped by a lighthouse-like little tower and a weather-vane in the shape of a prancing horse. This was the official residence of the *Landstallmeister*, or director. The family lived on the ground floor. Guests were taken up the broad wooden staircase from the hall to the first floor, where a huge dining room, adjacent sitting room and guest rooms overlooked the lovely park at the back. There paintings of Trakehner horses by well-known artists looked down on many a festive gathering. Ernst Ehlert and his wife Elisabeth, in the tradition of Trakehner *Landstallmeister*, were very hospitable. Lilli often saw government ministers, foreign diplomats, high-ranking officers and her grandfather's colleagues at table, and once even Prince Louis Ferdinand of Prussia, the grandson of Germany's last Kaiser. On some occasions

Ehlert had been a little too hospitable and invited more guests than there was room for, so he took to carrying a specific number of dried peas in his pocket at auctions, hunts or other social occasions. Each time he invited someone back for dinner he would take a pea from his pocket and drop it on the floor. When they were finished he – and his potential guests – knew that there were no more places for dinner, and he had to stop.

A warm-hearted and kindly man in his late 60s, Ehlert was a much-loved figure in Trakehnen, where the staff nicknamed him *Väterchen* – little father. Short and corpulent, with a large paunch and a greying moustache, he was not the most elegant *Landstallmeister* Trakehnen had seen, but he was greatly admired as an excellent manager of people and a brilliantly gifted breeder.

Ehlert presided over what was probably the largest stud farm in Europe, perhaps the world. For Trakehnen and its 16 outlying farms were spread out over 15,300 hectares to the north and, mostly, the south of the Reichsstrasse 1, the east-west highway which Napoleon had built to take his armies from Königsberg through Insterburg, Gumbinnen and across the border to Russia and Moscow. It looked like some vast well-tended park, with its meadows dotted with copses and clumps of bushes, ponds, gardens and groups of mostly red-brick buildings, and criss-crossed by neat, white-painted fences and long avenues of huge, ancient trees. And everywhere, swishing their tails, grazing, with foals gambolling around and black and white storks striding and pecking among them, were the near-legendary Trakehner horses.

Lilli would never have guessed that here was one of the most insecure, war-ravaged spots in Europe, whose inhabitants' parents, grandparents and great-grandparents had had to flee their homes. She could hardly tell that 86 of Trakehnen's buildings had been rebuilt only around 20 years earlier, after being destroyed by the Russians in the Great War. For the Horses' Paradise, as it was often called, exuded a sense of calm and permanence. It was a model stud farm, smooth-running and well-organised, where every employee, from the *Landstallmeister* down to the newest stable boy, knew his place and exactly what he had to do. It was not an opulent or ostentatious place – on the contrary, it was run with traditional Prussian simplicity and thriftiness. And in the old Prussian tradition, too, the staff were intensely proud to work there, as had their fathers and grandfathers before them, and treated the state's horses with the same love and care as if they were their own. In Germany and indeed many other countries, Trakehnen was spoken of with deep respect, even reverence. Lilli felt greatly privileged to be living in the middle of it all.

The *Hauptgestüt*, or main state stud farm, lay at the south-east corner of the area. When Lilli stepped out of the main door of the Schloss she would see straight in front of her a large, well-kept lawn with a huge and beautiful oak tree standing in the middle and in front of it, on a plinth, the life-size bronze model of the great stallion Tempelhüter. The statue, by the well-known equestrian artist Reinhold Kuebart, brother of the stud's resident architect, had been unveiled in 1931, shortly after her grandfather took up his post. It was the 200th anniversary of the founding of Trakehnen and Tempelhüter himself, by then 28 years old, was present. It had taken the place of the statue of another great sire, the chestnut Morgenstrahl, also by Kuebart, which had been taken by the Russians in booty after they invaded Trakehnen during the First World War.

To her right were the stables inhabited by a team of splendid glossy black Trakehners. Traditionally, the *Landstallmeister*'s carriages had always been drawn by black horses and with the drivers sitting ramrod-straight in their top hats and blue tail-coats, their whips held at a jaunty angle, they cut an impressive figure as they drove round the estate or picked up honoured guests at the station. The Trakehnen vets' carriages were drawn by chestnuts. Further along was the coach house, so that transport could be provided at a moment's notice. To her left, and left again round the corner of the Schloss, was the main drive which passed under a black and white arch, a famous Trakehnen landmark, on which was painted the elk's antler, and the date – 1732 – of the founding of Trakehnen. A few steps further on she could see the lovely park with a lily pond and, in the distance, the gardeners' yard. Turning right she would soon hear the sound of rushing water as she crossed a bridge over the little river Rodupp as it cascaded on to many large boulders which had been assembled there. The Rodupp, a pretty little river with gardens and large, overhanging trees on its steep banks, ran through the middle of the *Hauptgestüt*. On the bridge was a sluice to regulate the flow of the water, perhaps a reminder of Trakehnen's origins as marshland. A few kilometres further down, the Roddup ran into the river Pissa.

A few more steps, passing a large carp pond, on her right, and she was at the Triangle, the geographical centre of the Trakehnen. It was simply a point where three roads met, delineated on each of the three sides by rustic wooden fences. Straight in front of her was another huge and ancient oak, possibly older than Trakehnen itself. Slightly to its left was the Hotel Elch, with the glassed-in veranda of its dining room festooned with Virginia creeper. It was often full of life, for it was here that horsemen, breeders, international visitors, members of high society, officers, and many other guests would stay during the twice-weekly hunts, the twice-yearly auctions, the balls and other equestrian or social events. Further to the left, along the road leading to Trakehnen station, was the chemist's shop, a school and another oak tree, under which the school bus would be waiting to take her and other older children to the station in the morning. If, instead, she turned right at the Triangle, she would pass the architect's house, the stud's own post office and the blacksmith's house. Immediately beyond this was the smithy itself, with the smoke rising from its chimney and its apprentices learning the trade. On her right was the gigantic storehouse, several storeys high, where fodder was kept and next to it the flourmill. This was the beginning of a whole area of artisans, for just beyond was the locksmith's shop, the carpenter's shop, the sawmill, the mechanics' workshop, a barn and the stables for the 250 oxen and 450 farm horses – most of Trakehner descent – which worked the land. For nearly half of the stud land was given over to agriculture to feed both the 1,100 horses and the human population. The stud was self-sufficient in fodder and in much of the food needed by its inhabitants who, in the East Prussian farming tradition, received a sizeable part of their wages in kind – not only food, but firewood, housing and hens, cows and pigs to keep on their own patches of land.

Behind the storehouse was the office from which the farming in Trakehnen was directed, the cashier's office and the secretariat. Dotted around among all the stables, barns, workshops and offices were houses, single ones like the vets', or two, four or six-roomed houses for humbler members of staff, usually hidden among trees and bushes. Many of these had their own kitchen gardens and orchards and outhouses for their farm animals. In Trakehnen the staff usually lived just by, if not immediately above, the horses they cared for, or the benches or desks where they worked.

If she turned her back to the storehouse, Lilli could see along a soft, well-raked drive, lined on each side by gardens, footpaths and two stately rows of huge trees. At the end of this splendid avenue a low white, ivy-covered building about 100 metres long looked for all the world like another Schloss. And indeed it might, because it was the home of Trakehnen's great sires, among them Pythagoras, Termit, Cornut, Polarstern, Hyperion, Hellespont, Hirtensang and the young Keith.

These splendid stallions were the kings of Trakehnen. The roomy loose boxes in the sires' stables were only their winter residences. For the summer each had his own 'villa' or ivy-clad pavillion nearby, to shelter from the sun or rain, standing in its own spacious paddock surrounded by thick fir trees, where he could gallop around at will and relax after the exertions of the mating season. To the left of the sires' stables was the paddock where Tempelhüter spent many years. These 20 paddocks took up a large proportion of the *Hauptgestüt* and were a privilege that reflected the sires' status in the whole breeding system. They were also, it must be said, dictated by necessity: the stallions could not be put with the mares; if kept together they would fight and injure each other. Their paddocks were surrounded by double fencing, so none could reach his rival next door.

The pampered life of the sires, compared to those of the brood mares, was a reflection of the breeding system itself. Breeders knew, in fact, that mares' genes determined the qualities of their offspring as much as, and probably more than, those of the stallions. But one sire could serve scores – even hundreds – of mares, whereas a mare could produce at the most one foal a year, so his genes were quantitively more important to the breed and were selected with the greatest of care. And it was sires that Trakehnen existed to breed, not only sires for the *Hauptgestüt* itself, but ones that would be sent out to the four East Prussian *Landgestüte* to serve the farmers and private breeders' mares and thus would be responsible for the ever-improving quality of East Prussia's pedigree horses. Thus the sires were the stars of Trakehnen and the days when stallions were chosen to be sires and stallion parades were principal events in the Trakehner calendar.

The sires started their careers at the age of two and a

half, when they were picked out from their companions by Dr Ehlert and his expert colleagues, or bought from private breeders, and sent to the stallion testing centre at Zwion, 8 kilometres west of Georgenburg. There they were first ridden and driven in, and then given intensive endurance training over obstacle courses. It all ended with three-day tests in the field, but it was not only this that decided their futures. Throughout the training the experts had been gauging the way they moved, their temperament, health, energy levels and feeding habits. The year-long trials were not so much to select the best, but to weed out those that did not reach the extremely high standard in one way or another. On average about one-tenth were failed, castrated and sold off as riding horses.

But not even success in Zwion was enough to become a star. That would only come with time and offspring. For a great sire had to be a good progenitor, able to pass on his outstanding qualities to many sons and daughters. Of these the brightest star of the moment was the dark brown Pythagoras, grandson of Tempelhüter and great-grandson of Perfectionist. His son Totilas, also dark brown, was born the year Lilli came to Trakehnen and would go on to make Trakehner history. There was the chestnut Hyperion, a son of Dampfross and his own son Termit, whose mother was a daughter of Tempelhüter. There was the beautiful grey Fetysz, born in Poland of Arab blood, and Pilger, brown, another son of Tempelhüter.

Above the sires' stables was a small museum where visitors could see, among many other things, the skeletons of Perfectionist, the great Thoroughbred brought from England, and the mare Teichrose, who bore him Tempelhüter. They were a reminder to visitors that good bones and muscles, which the outsider does not see, are an important concern in breeding. Behind the stables was the centre, in a way, of the stud's whole life: the mating stable where each sire would be coupled, under close and expert supervision, with mares selected extremely carefully on the basis of their genealogy and characteristics.

The main mares' stables were not far away, along another tree-lined avenue. The horses at the main stud were divided into five herds: black; brown; chestnut; a mixed herd, which included greys, dun-coloured and piebald ones; and a fifth herd of heavier, farming horses. The chestnut herd, which had produced winners in two Olympic games, was kept at the main stud. Opposite and parallel to the mares' stables were the stables – the maternity ward, as it were – where the foals were born. It also served as a hospital for sick or injured horses, and behind was a small area where the convalescents would be put out for gentle exercise.

Mares, too, were subjected to strenuous tests. The majority of Trakehner mares were owned by farmers and had to work for their living as well as produce foals. But in recent years the Studbook Society had developed stringent tests involving four hours at the plough, two-in-hand, with each horse pulling an equivalent of 120 kg. This was followed two hours later by a 25-kilometre stint on a hard road pulling a load of 2,500 kg at a minimum of 11 kilometres an hour, then 30 minutes later, a riding test under the saddle, walking trotting and galloping over 2 kilometres in a minimum of two minutes 30 seconds. These tests were very much more demanding than the daily work normally required of farmers' mares, but helped to establish the strongest brood mares so that, when paired with the stallions, they would reproduce their qualities in their offspring. Trakehnen mares were subjected to similar tests, though without the ploughing. Little did the breeding experts imagine that before very long this inbred strength and toughness was about to be tested to its absolute limits in real life. Among the most successful mares to be tested was Ita, who belonged to Franz Scharffetter. Ita had produced a daughter, Italia, who was shortly to demonstrate what she was made of.

If Lilli walked on past the mares' stables and turned left, passed more sires' paddocks and then turned left again, she would come to another important cluster of stables, in dark-red brick and a vaguely Gothic style, like most of Trakehnen buildings. First was the auction stables where three-year-old Trakehners that were not required for breeding purposes were kept before being sold off in public auctions. Just because these horses had not been chosen for breeding did not mean they were in any way of poor quality – in fact they were very much in demand, particularly as riding horses.

Not far away were the stables of the yearling stallions. At a right angle to the auction stables was the huge, indoor riding arena and further on the long, low hunting stables, about 150 metres long. Here, as in the other stables, each horse would have its name on an ornate board over the sliding door of the box, followed by the names of its sire and dam. And here in the summer months three-year-old mares and geldings were trained for riding, eventing and show jumping, prior to being sold at the auctions.

Here, too, were the horses for the world-famous Trakehner hunts. These had been started at the beginning of the century by the then *Landstallmeister*, Burchard von Oettingen, who had also installed, at his own expense, the Trakehnen pack of hounds. The purpose was to put Trakehnen's products to the most stringent of tests and to develop and show off their remarkable abilities. Trakehnen's vast grounds were ideal: more than 350 fixed obstacles were laid out over an area of around 61,200 hectares of beautiful countryside, meadows, pastures and fields, so that the trail could be varied almost endlessly. There were wide and deep ditches, walls, fences and difficult combinations of all these. The stallions from Zwion were tested over these courses. The Trakehner steeplechases were even tougher than the hunts, open only to selected horses. The most important one was the 6,200-metre Von der Goltz Memorial Cup, which was considered the second most difficult obstacle race in the world after the Pardubice steeplechase in what was then Czechoslovakia. It was hardly surprising that between the wars, Trakehners had won the Pardubice steeplechase nine times.

The hunts attracted many expert riders from far and wide, prospective buyers of horses, officers from nearby regiments, as well as snobs, society figures and political and military bosses. The stable boys once spotted Field Marshal Wilhelm Keitel with a bevy of young ladies. *Reichsmarschall* Hermann Göring, Hitler's deputy, was often there, and when he went hunting on the nearby Rominten Heath he would order Ehlert to send him two coachmen and the best coach horses from his stables. Some visitors were arrogant and conceited and fancied themselves as superb riders. Those whose riding skills were in doubt were given quieter, utterly reliable steeds such as Tribut, an elderly black, but even then at the first serious hazard many ended up spreadeagled on the ground. The Trakehnen staff, who were infinitely better riders and never gave themselves airs, often found it hard to keep a straight face.

In front of the hunting stables was an open arena with a small ornate pavilion in the middle like a little summerhouse, which had once served as a council chamber for the judges during the selection of sires. Opposite the hunting stables, just behind the *Landstallmeister*'s coach-house were the kennels of the Trakehnen hounds, with their own open yard surrounded by a high wall with a small tower at one corner from which the master of hounds could survey his pack. Set a short distance away from the auction stables, but easy to find because of its pungent smell, was the foxes' pen. The foxes were there not to be hunted, but to produce the droppings in which the drag was rolled before it was trailed across the countryside with hounds and riders in hot pursuit. The routes were made more and more difficult as the hunting season went on and the hounds, horses and riders became faster and fitter.

The hunting stables were the realm of *Obersattelmeister* Kiaulehn, a gruff, balding man with gold-rimmed spectacles who was a force to be reckoned with in Trakehnen. He was the chief groom in charge of the horses in both the hunting stables and the auction stables, as well as the 40 or 50 stable boys, upon whom he imposed a strict but fair discipline – doubtless a legacy from the 12 years he had served in the army. But the respect or fear he commanded in Trakehnen was also due also to his political role, for he was the *Ortsgruppenführer*, the Nazi Party boss in the stud and its village, and the local mayor as well. He lived in an apartment above the stables. He seems to have been more of a loyal, solid old Trakehnen horseman that a Nazi fanatic, and it is possible that Ehlert asked him to take on the role to prevent some undesirable figure from being sent in from outside.

Opposite Kiaulehn's stables, across the arena, was a red-brick building where the stable boys lived. Otto Fiege and Helmut Hufenbach, like many young lads in the area, had wanted nothing more than to work in Trakehnen. At the age of 14, once they had finished their eight years of compulsory schooling and had been confirmed, they were sent, scrubbed, brushed and combed, to Kiaulehn for an interview. Before the war, practically only the sons of grooms or other members of staff were accepted, but now so many men over 18 had been drafted into the armed forces that Kiaulehn was employing boys like Fiege and Hufenbach, who came from villages a little further afield. Experience with horses and ability to ride were a great advantage. Hufenbach had grown up among horses that his grandfather and father had owned and was readily accepted.

The boys that were chosen were sent with their

bedding and a few belongings to the stable boys' house to start at the bottom end of an almost military hierarchy that would last three years, ending with an examination and promotion to the rank of groom. Under normal circumstances they would become Prussian civil servants after 12 years spent rising through the various ranks in the stud, with all the security and privileges that this brought. But this was wartime and all knew that at 18 they would have to go to war, possibly never to return.

For the moment, however, they were put in the novices' room below the gable, where about a dozen of them slept on wooden beds and sacks of straw. The youngest boys would be made to sleep furthest away from the stove, moving closer with time and graduating next to a more privileged room. After a couple of years they would be allowed to sleep on proper mattresses and even, if they were the oldest, next to the stove. In the stables the same hierarchy prevailed, with the newcomers getting the lowliest jobs, such as gathering the droppings of the mares and their foals so that the young foals would not eat them.

Their day would begin at six in the morning with a bell. In winter it was still dark and lights would go on in the cold stables as the boys clattered down the stone stairs and into the boxes. Each had two horses to look after. They would fetch their charges' oats and hay and buckets of water from the pump, and give them the first meal of the day. Then they would run upstairs again to wash, dress properly in their green working uniform with Russian-style high-collared jackets, caps and boots, and have their own breakfast. Then down again and into the saddle to break in, ride and jump the young horses that were destined to be sold off.

Besides feeding the horses four times a day, riding and other tasks, they had to don aprons and clean out the stables, groom the horses till they shone, clean the harness and rake the sandy paths carefully into patterns so that they looked almost like carpets. They had to learn to deal gently and skilfully with spirited and unbroken young horses – woe betide any stable boy caught hitting a horse! They had to learn to recognise each horse in the stud and know its name, as if it were a person. They were required to learn the ancestry of each one off by heart and when it was their turn to look after the weaned foals that did not yet have names, they needed to know exactly who its father and mother were. An unpopular chore was night duty at the stables, when one boy had to keep watch till dawn in case a horse fell sick or an accident happened, whereupon he was supposed to call the *Obersattelmeister* from his apartment above.

There were many challenges to their new skills, such as the heart-rending day when the foals were about five months old and had to be separated from their mothers and taken to their own stables and pastures – a difficult job with the mothers neighing and thrashing around indignantly and the foals crying pitifully. Or the day when the young horses were around three years old and were taken from the outlying farms where they had grazed and played and were brought into the hunting stables to be broken in and face the realities of a horse's life. They would rear and plunge wildly and try to tear away, and once in the boxes would kick about, neighing frantically and bouncing against the walls. The next morning, before they were fully awake, two stable boys would go into each box, get a saddle on the horse and drag it out, protesting violently, to the arena, where they would all be let loose and driven round and round until they were tired. Then the lighter of the two stable boys was heaved into the saddle and – in scenes worthy of the Wild West – had to try and stay on, without stirrups, while the other hung on to the leading rein.

Four dozen-odd teenage boys were quite a handful and Kiaulehn had a repertoire of penalties for misdemeanours. A frequent punishment was the night watch in the stables. Boys who failed to turn up at the Hitler Youth meetings would find themselves on Sunday afternoons (their only free afternoon) with metal hooks in their hands, prising out weeds from the cracks between the paving stones in front of the *Landstallmeister*'s Schloss. When one day all the apples were found to have vanished from the apple trees in the orchard of the Hotel Elch, a search of the stable boys' cupboards was ordered and of course apples rolled out all over the floor. Trakehnen folk were treated to the sight of a procession of 17 stable boys with sacks of apples on their backs being marched on foot through the village to the police station, with the local policeman on a horse in front and Kiaulehn riding at the rear.

Kiaulehn was not popular with his charges. At least once they got their revenge: riding back to the stud one day with Kiaulehn leading the way on his beautiful grey, Ponza, the boys gradually dropped back and then at a signal, suddenly sped their horses up and closed in on the grey. Ponza, unnerved, shot off ahead and Kiaulehn thumped onto the road in a cloud of dust. The *Obersattelmeister* was not amused.

For all the smooth efficiency of the place, Dr Ehlert's day was a busy one and he had to cover large distances to keep an eye on what was going on in the outlying farms. Lilli loved accompanying her grandfather on his rounds. As the *Landstallmeister*'s carriage arrived at a stable or a farm, the man in charge would stand to attention, help Ehlert down from the carriage and report on the situation. Lilli had to stay where she was so as not, she suspected, to interrupt discussions with her many questions. When her grandfather returned to the carriage she could tell from his face whether all was going well or whether there were problems.

In winter they would do the rounds in a sleigh, with bells ringing merrily as they went. The horses' shoes were fitted with pointed studs to prevent them slipping, the coachman would be wrapped in a voluminous fur-lined coat, her grandfather wore a fur coat and Lilli had a footmuff to keep her feet warm.

Ten of Trakehnen's outlying farms lay in a half-circle some distance away and four more were much further to the north, beyond the main road and the railway line. Another, Bajohrgallen, was nearby, between Trakehnen and its station. To the west, some 15 kilometres along an oak-lined avenue, was Mattischken, where the most promising young stallions were sent because the grazing was particularly good and gave them the best possible nutrition. The black mares and their foals lived in Gurdzen. They were slightly heavier than the others and perhaps the most aesthetically pleasing of all Trakehners, with their shiny coats of the deepest possible black.

Everyone here knew the story of how the beauty of the blacks once saved Trakehnen. During the Seven Years' War (1756–63) East Prussia fell temporarily under Russian occupation. As a precaution, *Landstallmeister* von Domhardt had sent the sires and his most valuable mares to Berlin and elsewhere, and instructed their grooms to treat them as if they were their own, for in those times Russian troops respected private property. But when the Russian commander, General Nikolaus von Korff, started to take an interest in the stud, von Domhardt feared that his precious horses would end up in Russia. So he took the bull by the horns and invited the General to visit Trakehnen and be his guest in the Schloss. There ensued a merry evening with doubtless much to drink and plenty of horse stories to tell. The next day, as they were about to set out to tour the stud, von Domhardt had a selection of blacks paraded in front of the Schloss. As intended, the General fell into such raptures about the beautiful animals that von Domhardt promptly presented them to him as a gift. The Russian was so delighted that the tour and any other plans he may have had were forgotten. He went away happy and the rest of the Trakehners, and particularly the priceless sires, were safe.

The brown herd were kept on Kalpakin farm. They were also very elegant, with their darker legs, manes and tails, and among them were many descendants of Perfectionist and Tempelhüter. One of these was Nurmi, one of the winners of the 1936 Berlin Olympics.

But the first horses that a visitor would see on approaching the Trakehnen were the mixed herd that lived in Bajohrgallen and whose grazing meadows lay along the road from the station to the stud itself. 'Mixed' did not mean second-class – for this herd included some of the finest horses of all, including some pure thoroughbreds and Arabs. Outstanding among them were the greys, which the uninitiated call white horses (pure white horses, which have pink skin and blue eyes, are rare; most have darker skins and the coat is often not entirely white). This had been the herd of the internationally famous grey sire Cancara, himself the son of an equally famous father, the Anglo-Arab Nana Sahib. Cancara's place had been taken in recent years by the beautiful grey Fetysz from Poland, a horse so graceful he reminded one of a unicorn. Fetysz passed on his snowy coat to many of his children, which is often not the case with grey sires. As Lilli arrived in Trakehnen, three female foals had just been born in that herd that were to play vital roles for the future of the whole breed in the years to come. Two of them were Cancara's daughters, Donna and Kokette; the third was Kassette.

IN THE MIDDLE of June 1941 Hitler and his staff left Berlin and took up position in the Wolf's Lair. The conquest of the east was about to begin.

CHAPTER 4

'They that sow the wind ...'

At 3.30 in the morning of 22 June 1941, all hell broke loose. Aircraft roared and screamed overhead, bombs fell. A bomb exploded close to Lenken; others killed stallions in the army depot near Ragnit. Soldiers were marching eastwards across the border. The scores of Wehrmacht horses that had been crammed into stables, barns and all available buildings on the estate of Sabloczyn close to the Polish border suddenly disappeared with them. Trakehnen's farms were shaking to the rumble of tanks and military vehicles surging eastwards along Napoleon's highway to Russia – exactly 129 years to the day since Napoleon and his armies had set out on on their own ill-fated expedition to Moscow.

Hitler's invasion of the Soviet Union had begun. Johanna Sasse, daughter of Max Haedge-Medicus and chatelaine of Sabloczyn, understood the lessons of history: she knew from that moment that her homeland was doomed.

The German army, Hitler fancied, was about to complete the work that the Teutonic Knights had started 600 years earlier. In a snappy, 10-week campaign it was going to drive the Red Army beyond the Urals, set up a line of defence from Archangelsk in the north to the

Volga River and create space to expand – *Lebensraum* – for the German people. This was to be an important part of his future Europe-wide Empire, to be ruled by the German Master Race. Germans would take possession of the rich raw materials: coal, iron ore, the forests and the vast wheat fields of Ukraine, solve all their economic problems and roll in plenty. 'The German colonist ought to live on handsome, spacious farms. The German services will be lodged in marvellous buildings, the governors in palaces …', he once boasted during private talks. 'Around the city, to a depth of thirty to forty kilometres we shall have a belt of handsome villages connected by the best roads …' The fate of the original population was of no concern. Slavs, Hitler said, were sub-humans – *Untermenschen* – who had no right to exist, except as slaves to the Master Race. Bureaucrats in Berlin had worked out that many millions of Russians, Belorussians, Ukrainians and others, would starve to death as a result of these plans. No one there saw anything to object to in that.

The war in the east was to be nothing like that in the west, which, apart from a number of horrific exceptions, was conducted more or less according to international conventions. In the east, Hitler freed his troops of any obligation to observe international law. War crimes would be excused. Communist political commissars were to be liquidated. Enemy civilians could be shot without trial on an officer's order. 'The war against Russia,' Hitler told his generals, 'will be such that it cannot be conducted in a chivalrous fashion. This struggle is one of ideologies and racial differences and will have to be conducted with unprecedented, unmerciful and unrelenting harshness. All officers will have to rid themselves of obsolete ideologies. I know that the necessity for such means of waging war is beyond the comprehension of you generals but … I insist absolutely that my orders be executed without contradiction.'

Three million German troops invaded the Soviet Union on a broad front reaching south from East Prussia to Romania. With them were 3,350 tanks, 500 aircraft, 7,000 pieces of artillery and 750,000 horses, many of them Trakehners. Peter Elxnat's Horse Artillery unit, which had already seen action in Poland and on the Belgian border, was in Bordeaux when the Russian campaign began. It was ordered to set off for the Polish-Soviet border on the river Bug, on horseback as ever, and later continued as far as the Volga. Years later he was to estimate that the distances he had travelled on his Trakehner mounts, or walked by their side to relieve them for a while, could have encircled the globe several times. It was on marches such as these that Trakehners really lived up to their reputation as the best soldiers' horse in the world, for they could march long distances, rarely became lame or sick, could recover quickly from exhaustion and exist on very little fodder. And unlike their predecessors in the traditional cavalry, the modern Trakehners had to carry not only a soldier but also 150 kilograms' worth of modern arms, equipment and baggage. It was at such times, also, that Elxnat and his comrades knew exhaustion such as they had never experienced before. Sometimes they had to march for 20 or even 22 hours consecutively, and the remaining hours were not for sleeping. First they had to forage for grass, hay, oats and water for the horses. They would often fall asleep as they rode, bolt upright in the saddle.

It was a long way from traditional cavalry warfare. The German cavalry regiments had put their three-metre-long steel lances away in 1927 and most units, but not all, carried sabres only on ceremonial occasions. The classic cavalry charge of past centuries was now – almost, but not quite – history. During the invasion of Poland, Polish cavalry had wiped out a German infantry battalion in a lance charge (reports that the Poles charged tanks with lances appear to be a myth, possibly created by German propaganda) and, astonishingly, several sabre battles took place, although none of these were decisive and were generally ignored by military historians. Now they were called Mounted Regiments and the mounts of some of them were not horses but humble bicycles. But the mobility provided by horses was invaluable. Armed with machine guns and their own horse-drawn artillery, the mounted troops were used as a rapid-reaction force that would intervene quickly in a situation, and then move on rapidly to another. Mounted troops were much used for reconnaissance and for crossing rivers fast, long before the sappers could build bridges, since horses are good swimmers.

Mounted soldiers, who were good riders and experienced horsemen, maintained the cavalry tradition of treating their horses with care, kindness and respect. Whatever else may have happened in the war, the army's horses were well treated.

Horses were essential in the Russian campaign:

German industry had not been able to produce enough vehicles and most infantry and artillery regiments had many horses to pull their weapons and equipment over difficult terrain. For in the Soviet Union, where paved roads were still few, vehicles would get stuck in mud or snow. They would frequently break down, radiators would freeze up and batteries fail, while the tough East Prussian horses would go on and on. But in the severe winter of 1941–2 a serious shortage of fodder arose, many horses died and the Peter Elxnat's unit was switched over to tanks. Shortly afterwards he was badly wounded in the knees and discharged.

The invasion of the Soviet Union was Erich Koch's great chance. He was made the *Reichskommissar*, or governor, of Ukraine. Since he remained Gauleiter of East Prussia, and had recently been put in charge of the neighbouring Polish districts of Bialystock and Ciechanow as well, his power now extended over a vast area from the Baltic to the Black Sea. His career was reaching unimagined heights, and his megalomania expanded accordingly. He appropriated princely Polish and Ukrainian palaces, renovated them for vast sums of money and held parties and hunts of feudal magnificence.

With a little skill and humanity Koch could easily have turned Ukraine into an ally of Germany. Many of the population had welcomed the arrival of the Germans as a hope of deliverance from the yoke of Stalin, and some had even volunteered to join the Wehrmacht, the German armed forces. Indeed, many Ukrainian Cossacks so hated the Reds that they fought on the side of the Germans.

Instead, he instituted a reign of terror and rapidly became the most loathed of all Hitler's viceroys in the east. He set about turning Ukraine into a slave nation. Its huge mineral resources, particularly coal and iron ore, and its rich agriculture were to be plundered. Its people, as far as he was concerned, were 'negroes'. In a notorious speech in Kiev he declared, 'we have truly not come here to spread manna around, we have come here to create the conditions for victory … We are a Master Race and must remember that the lowliest German worker is racially and biologically worth a thousand times more than the population here.' His first move had been to close down all schools, declaring that Ukrainian children had no need of education; the Germans would teach them all they needed to know. He persecuted and deported the Jews. He publicly declared that his aim was the decimation of the Ukrainian intelligentsia. He had the populations of whole towns and villages rounded up and shipped off, often without food, water or sanitary arrangements, in railway wagons to Germany to work as slaves in industry and agriculture. He had tens of thousands of innocent people thrown into jails and concentration camps. Pleased with his own work, he put it about that he would soon be the Gauleiter of Moscow.

Within a short time he had turned the entire population against him and the forests were soon teeming with partisans who harassed and fought the German troops.

On 19 November 1941, Hitler, who was relaxing with some of his generals at his Alpine retreat near Berchtesgaden, received a telephone called from his eastern headquarters at the Wolf's Lair. In a blizzard at dawn that morning the Soviet army had launched a counteroffensive against the 285,000-strong German Sixth Army besieging a small but tenacious Soviet force holding part of Stalingrad. The Soviets were driving in great strength from the north and the south to encircle the Germans. The Sixth Army's only hope of survival was to break out quickly. Hitler, who was obsessed with possessing Stalingrad, and had dismissed intelligence reports that vast and well-equipped Soviet forces were approaching, flatly refused. An attempt to relieve the encircled forces whose men were starving and freezing to death, failed. Twice the Soviet Army offered the besieged generals an honourable surrender, with food for the troops and medical treatment for the innumerable wounded. But twice Hitler flatly refused. The Sixth Army would fight to the last man and the last round and by doing so would make an unforgettable contribution 'towards the establishment of a defensive front and the salvation of the Western world,' he declared.

At the beginning of February the Sixth Army had collapsed and 91,000 survivors, many wounded, were dragging themselves through ice and snow, in temperatures of minus 24 degrees, towards prisoner-of-war camps in Siberia. Most of the rest had perished. Only 5,000 of them were ever to see their homeland again.

The catastrophe inflicted by Hitler's insane obstinacy was portrayed to the German people as a heroic tragedy caused by the superiority of the enemy and 'unfavourable circumstances'. In fact it was the greatest and most humiliating defeat Germany had ever suffered and a major turning point in the war. Above all, it gave Stalin and the Soviet Union an immense psychological boost of confidence: they realised that the dreaded Germans were not, after all, invincible.

On 22 June 1944, three years to the day after the Wehrmacht invaded the Soviet Union, the Red Army began its vast offensive to drive the Germans out and put an end forever to the Nazis' dream of an empire in the east. And not only that: Stalin was determined to drive to the heart of the Reich and keep whole tracts of it for himself. After recapturing Minsk, Vilnius, Grodno and Kaunas, the Red Army headed for the German border.

Koch and his henchmen had fled Ukraine and soon he was ensconced back in East Prussia and embarking on new tasks. He was now not only Gauleiter but also *Reichsverteidigungskommissar* (State Defence Commissioner), responsible for the defence of his area. It was a task that Hitler, ever at odds with his generals, thought his eastern Gauleiters could do better. Koch threw himself into the formation of the *Volkssturm*, the people's militia, and the building of the *Ostwall*, or eastern bulwark, a line of fortifications from the Memel to Warsaw that was supposed to help keep the Russians out. The *Ostwall* was his project, built as he and his cronies thought fit. Koch shared his Führer's low opinion of the military and the army were only allowed, at the most, to give advice, which was often ignored. Two great anti-tank trenches were dug across the von Zitzewitzs' land at Weedern.

All men from 16 to 65 who, for whatever reason, were exempt from military call-up, were compelled to join the *Volkssturm*. They were taken off for three or four weeks at a time to dig the anti-tank ditches and fox-holes and build the bunkers along the *Ostwall* and to drill with their motley collection of weapons. In the Trakehnen area it was *Obersattelmeister* Kiaulehn who saw to it that every able-bodied man who was not in the army went off to do his stint.

Volkssturm duty was particularly damaging to farms and businesses that were already struggling to keep going in the absence of many male staff who had been called up. Absurdly, many farm workers were forced to do *Volkssturm* duty right at harvest time, and the army had to provide harvest battalions to help get the crops in. As those who had fought in the First World War could easily see, much of the *Ostwall* was of little military value. One farmer scoffed '*Ach*, don't talk to me about Koch and his *Wall*. The Russians will deal with that in three hours. It will take them two and a half hours to stop laughing at it and half an hour to climb over it.' A highly dangerous remark to make, but prophetic.

Drained of staff by the draft and the *Volkssturm*, German farmers and firms, particularly in the war industries, could hardly function without the nearly five million forced labourers – men, women, and children – and two million prisoners-of-war shipped into Germany from conquered lands to work. The vast majority were from the Soviet Union, but there were many Poles and French and some Dutch, Italians and Yugoslavs. The conditions in many industries and the camps where they were held – for those who had not already died of hunger, thirst or exposure on the way – were hellish, with little or no food and water, sanitation, sufficient shelter, clothing or rest. They were forced to work till they dropped. By comparison, those who were put to work on farms and in private homes were the lucky ones, even though the local Nazi bosses tried to make sure they were treated harshly. On the Scharffetters' farm a Pole was beaten up by Nazi thugs for having a relationship with a female forced labourer. At Lenken, Nazi thugs tried to take away a sick Russian woman and her two teenage children who had been working for the von Sperbers. After much argument Barbara finally persuaded them to let them stay in return for 10 eggs. When the small daughter of a Polish housemaid fell down the stairs and severely gashed her head, Johanna Sasse called a doctor. But the doctor looked at the girl, closed his bag and said, 'You did not tell me she was Polish. I do not treat Poles.' Furious, Johanna reminded him he had sworn the Hippocratic oath and told him never to come near her estate again. She took the girl to the local apothecary, who patched her up as best he could. In fact, behind the scenes on many farms and in many families the foreigners were treated with kindness – kindness that the foreigners were to repay many times over, often by saving their German employers' lives.

Trakehnen was different. Prisoners of war and forced labourers worked in its fields, producing the fodder. But none were used to care for the horses, perhaps because they would have lacked the necessary training. A few members of staff were exempted from call-up. But otherwise Ehlert had only men over 60 and teenage boys to run his vast stud farm.

CHAPTER 5

'The Trakehners can race against the Russian tanks'

As the Russians drew ever closer and Ernst Ehlert fretted, Berlin had not been idle. Seyffert had been putting pressure on the top figures in the ministry to let the Trakehnen horses go. The official reply was a flat 'no'. 'Under no circumstances' were horses to be moved westwards from Trakehnen and the other easterly state stud farms, he was told.

Unofficially, however, his superiors conceded that four or five of the most valuable sires and 'a few' mares could be sent to Graditz, a state stud farm near Torgau on the river Elbe, on condition that the public was told that this was a move to augment the local herd and that it had nothing to do with the war. Arrangements to evacuate Trakehnen, Georgenburg and Rastenburg, the two most endangered East Prussian stallion depots, could be 'only prepared mentally', he noted down afterwards. Seyffert, stretching this concession as far as he could, promptly despatched an emissary to Trakehnen and Georgenburg to inform Ehlert and Heling verbally how many horses were to be sent to which westerly stud farm. He sent copies of the plans to the other

Landstallmeister, prudently stamped 'secret' – it would not do for this information to get out. Seyffert also told Klein to arrange for Trakehnen's studbooks, the unique and extremely valuable records of the breed from its early days, to be sent to presumed safety at Neustadt on the Dosse, and at the same time have 10 to 15 brood mares quietly shipped to Neustadt under the pretext of 'reinforcing the Neustadt herd of brood mares'. It looked as if they might be able to rescue at least the most important horses by clever tactics.

But four days later Klein returned with bad news. They were being refused railway wagons to ship even those few horses out. Phone calls and pleas to top ministry officials were in vain. 'In the present situation there can be no question of evacuating East Prussian studs,' Seyffert was told.

THE WAR was drawing in on Trakehnen. At night the eastern sky was tinged red from explosions and the flames from burning towns. From time to time the whole stud was lit up as bright as day by the flares that preceded bomb attacks. By day Soviet aircraft would roar down over the paddocks and fire at the airfield and station, killing several civilians. They dropped small bombs, which luckily did little damage. Leaflets fluttered down from the planes, bearing an incongruous message: 'We don't want to harm Trakehnen because the poor horses need peace and quiet.' Women were unwilling to go out in the fields for fear of being shot at from the planes and it was uncertain whether they would be able to get the harvest in. As July drew to a close, near-panic gripped the population: word was spreading that the Soviets would invade on 3 August 1944. As it happened, the day passed uneventfully. Nevertheless the accounts given by soldiers returning from the front, who were intensively questioned by local people, were alarming. The Nazis' propaganda machine was churning out triumphalist predictions of victory, but the soldiers were telling them that the hopes of keeping the Soviets out were extremely slim.

An ever-growing stream of refugees was trudging in from the east. Pale, anxious, their belongings piled on carts; they had frightening stories to tell. Many of them were Germans whose ancestors had settled in countries to the east generations earlier. Local people looked at them and wondered whether they would soon be facing the same fate, and having to join the tragic procession. Most distressing were the ownerless animals – above all cows – that wandered in, unmilked and howling with pain from inflamed udders. They trampled down the fences and grazed, thousands at a time, on Trakehnen's meadows, eating them bare of the second crop of hay destined for the horses. The army seemed to be everywhere; officers and solders were billeted on Trakehnen families, even in the *Landstallmeister*'s Schloss.

Seyffert, frustrated that he was getting nowhere, travelled to Trakehnen and then on to Königsberg, where on 5 August he managed to speak to Koch personally. He explained that the stud was simply unable to function normally, its buildings and land were full of Wehrmacht units, low-flying planes were threatening horses and staff and there was a serious danger that the horses would be infected with diseases brought in by the refugees' livestock. Seyffert knew it would be futile to press for a complete evacuation, but begged to be allowed at least to bring some of the most valuable stallions out with Wehrmacht trains that were returning empty from the front. If the horses were not allowed to leave East Prussia, at least they could be housed in some more westerly military horse depots, he argued.

His efforts were in vain. Koch flatly refused to allow any horses out 'as long as there are women and children in the area'. Koch probably did not tell Seyffert that just at that time he was having the horses of his own private stables evacuated from his Polish palace in Krasne, near Ciechanow, and shipped westwards.

Before the Nazis' rise to power, the *Oberlandstallmeister* and the *Landstallmeister* of Trakehnen were authoritative, highly respected figures whose demands were heeded. Now everything was different, and it was clear that neither Seyffert nor Ehlert had the necessary influence within the Nazi Party, and particularly with Koch, to get things done. Darré, whose visions of making Germany self-sufficient in food had predictably failed, had been sacked and was living quietly in the Schorfheide forest, near Berlin. His successor, Herbert Backe, was another fanatical Nazi ideologue whose great aim had been to plunder the Soviet Union of food and use it to feed the Wehrmacht and the Germans back home, leaving millions to die of starvation. For him horses were a minor concern.

There was only one thing to do: go over Koch's head. Seyffert decided to appeal to Göring to override Koch's decision. He contacted Göring's chief aide, Dr Fritz Görrnert, who, among his various functions, was also commander of Göring's special train. Görrnert did what he could, but had to come back with the reply that 'the Reich Marshal does not feel he has the authority to issue such instructions to Gauleiter Koch, who as *Reichsverteidigungskommissar* has been invested with special powers by the Führer'.

Unperturbed, however, the helpful Görrnert went one better. He got in touch with Hitler's adjutant, Walter Bormann, and asked him to put the matter to the Führer himself. Hitler, Bormann reported back, 'quite understood' the *Oberlandstallmeister*'s problem. But in view of the special powers he had given Koch, the Führer said the matter would have to be sorted out between Koch and Minister Backe. Seyffert persuaded Backe to send an urgent telex message to Koch asking for permission to send 10 stallions and 100 brood mares to Graditz 'in order to guarantee the continuation of the centuries-old Trakehner breed at least on a limited scale'. He received no reply. Another telex was sent. Finally, 10 days later, a message from Koch was telexed, not to the Minister but to the East Prussian farmers' organisation, reiterating that the horses may not go 'as long as women and children remain in the area'. And Koch, needless to say, was not planning to evacuate women and children.

Suddenly a small ray of light appeared in the shape of a formal request from a 'Schorfheide Foundation' to buy 30 two-year-old mares that were not required for breeding. They were needed for agricultural work, it was explained. It turned out that the Foundation was a scheme devised by Göring, a passionate huntsman, to take over the beautiful Schorfheide forest near Berlin, which previously belonged to the Prussian forestry authorities, to populate it with all sorts of game and use it virtually as a personal hunting ground. The request for the horses was signed by the Foundation's chairman, who was none other than the obliging Dr Görrnert. Whether the Foundation really needed 30 young horses or whether Göring and Görrnert simply wanted to save some Trakehners while bypassing the detested Koch, was not clear and probably of little interest to Seyffert. The crucial point as far as he was concerned was that Görrnert was putting at his disposal more railway wagons than were actually needed – the remaining space was at Ehlert's disposal to smuggle out a number of valuable brood mares, which would be dropped off at Neustadt. Seyffert urged Ehlert to send the old studbooks along with them.

Back in Trakehnen the situation was becoming critical. As Ehlert had feared, some of his horses, particularly the yearling mares, had caught infections from either the refugees' horses or those of the Wehrmacht. But there was worse. On 22 August Ehlert poured out all his problems to Seyffert in a letter that betrayed his state of agitation.

> Dear Oberlandstallmeister!
> As you will have learned from the Wehrmacht reports, the military situation on this front remains serious, and above all, uncertain. A few days ago the *Ortsgruppenleiter* passed on for my information plans by the

Rural District Office at Ebenrode (Stallupönen) in case we should have to evacuate. They stipulate that horses should be driven out last, that is, after herds of cattle etc. Since that is clearly impossible I drove immediately to the District Administrator who saw the point, but did not feel he had the authority to make any fundamental changes.

Whereupon I discussed the situation and above all my proposals to ship the horses out once again with Henninges [*probably his former assistant Jürgen von Henninges*] and asked him to drive by car (since there are hardly any trains here now) to District President Hoffmann in Königsberg since he has been told by the Gauleiter to prepare the ground for a possible evacuation. Even there he achieved little. We are supposed to have the *right* to leave before the cattle, and *in case of danger* 12 sires and around 100 mares can be sent away, if possible, by rail. The application for this is thought to have come from the Ministry. But whether this can be achieved in the face of imminent danger – in other words, if the front moves closer, seems very doubtful. I am supposed to be informed in writing about these points, but this has not happened yet.

Moreover I am having a *great deal of trouble* with the herds of strange cattle, each several thousand strong, which moved in some three weeks ago and have not only eaten away all the grass and broken down the fences but have also caused considerable damage to the grain and the root crops. In a few weeks' time our herds will have to be brought in and

> then there will not be enough hay, especially since the second crop has been destroyed by these cattle.
>
> It is also not particularly pleasant that the airfield immediately next to the Trakehnen parade paddock has now been in use for several days. There is naturally a great danger of big night attacks and it has not meant any reduction in daylight strafing raids. If I could only send away the 12 sires and some 100 mares, I could at least clear the most vulnerable stables of the chestnut herd. As things are, it can't be done and I can only hope the Russian airmen will spare them …

Still no permission came through. A week later, in desperation, he telephoned the Gauleiter's office and pleaded with Koch personally. Koch's response was staggering: 'If the Russians should advance temporarily, the Trakehners can prove their mettle by racing against the Soviet tanks.'

With great self-control Ehlert replied calmly that on an open road the brood mares – as long as they were not pregnant – and the fillies would doubtless pass this test. But he pointed out that the roads would certainly be jammed with treks, which, along with the mares, would be scattered by the wilder sires and young stallions.

It worked. Koch agreed that the sires and some of the best pregnant mares should be shipped to safety.

Armed at last with Koch's consent, Ehlert lost no time. An army quartermaster had been billeted in the Schloss and Ehlert asked him to get him a train that was returning empty from the front, to which he willingly agreed. Koch had now agreed to let 15 sires and around 100 brood mares go. Thus the star stallions Pythagoras, Termit, Cornut, Fetysz and others headed for presumed safety. With them, Ehlert noted, were 'the most proven mares and the best of the fillies, so that now come what may, a stock of Trakehner blood is safe'.

But if any of the Gauleiter's spies had counted the horses on the train that pulled out of Trakehnen station on 2 September 1944, they would have found not 100 but 139 mares. They would also have found a chest full of old documents and two chests containing most of the valuable oil paintings of star Trakehner sires and mares, which had looked down on many a *Landstallmeister*'s dinner party in the dining room of the Schloss.

The war of attrition continued. On the evening of 7 September, Kiaulehn brought good news: they had permission to send out more horses. Ehlert, with the help of the excellent stationmaster at Trakehnen, ordered a large number of wagons intending to despatch some 350 mares and foals to various other studs. But the next morning came a phone call from the District Administrator: the Gauleiter had forbidden any further evacuation, either by rail or on foot. Moreover he was demanding a list of the horses that had already been sent. Furthermore, the District Administrator went on, it was strictly forbidden to ship any kind of fodder out of the province. Since the other studs did not have sufficient fodder for the new arrivals, there was obviously no point in sending them. The wagons had to be cancelled.

EVERY AUTUMN all the *Landstallmeister* of the Prussian stud farms – Heling from Georgenburg, Wilhelm Uppenborn from Rastenburg, Hermann-Wilhelm von Warburg from Braunsberg and Hans Ehlers from Marienwerder – would gather in Trakehnen for the distribution of the two-and-a-half-year-old colts among their studs. It was always a jolly, convivial event in which they would compete, with all the tricks and cunning they could muster, to get the best young stallions for their own stud. This business over, they would spend a merry evening in the Schloss. This year the meeting had been brought forward to the first half of September because of the feared invasion and, as Martin Heling recalled later, 'the usual humorous note was missing and in a subdued mood we tussled hard with each other but did not quite find the old jocular tone. We were refusing perhaps to admit to ourselves that this was the last time, we had a foreboding of an inexorable fate which was poised to deal a final blow.' As they parted with heavy hearts, the *Landstallmeister* knew that they might never see Trakehnen again.

A few days later Koch's order was reversed again: Ehlert could now send out around 200 young horses and foals. But he had to wait some days before wagons became available again. Finally on 16 September the wagons arrived and the animals were just being loaded on to the train when another phone call came. Permission had been rescinded; the horses must not go. After much argument minds were changed yet again and the horses went, leaving Ehlert and his staff with their nerves in shreds.

Meanwhile the orders that Ehlert had been waiting for in vain were received over in Lenken. The 10-kilometre zone inside the border – and that alone – was to be cleared. Barbara von Sperber was told they must leave that very day. But 13 wagons had to be lengthened to carry the families and their essential belongings, people had to pack, much needed to be organised and the trek did not leave until the next day. She had already been able to send part of her herd away, but 38 extremely valuable pedigree horses remained and Barbara left a note on her writing desk asking whoever found it – she assumed it would be army officers – to have them shipped to her family's home in Nauendorf, near Oschatz in Saxony. At first Barbara led the trek on horseback, but after a couple of days, perhaps unnerved by the slow progress on the roads, her horse lost its nerve and bolted. She fell, relatively luckily as it happened, because the horse ended up in a pond, badly injured. Shortly after they set off, his senior officer gave her husband leave so that he could join them and lead the trek.

To the south-east, in Uszpiaunehmen, the Pflaumbaums were also leaving. The local Brownshirts had fled, there was no one now to stop them and the army officers billeted on the house, who were only too aware of the danger, urged them to go. But before they set off there was important business to attend to. Brigitte Pflaumbaum and Heinz Boettcher, one of the officers, went to the Standesamt and got married. It was hardly a joyous affair, with the wagons packed, and fear of the future hanging over them. The electricity had failed but Brigitte's mother baked them a cake over the fire. The couple celebrated with a toast with Brigitte's parents, her sister Vera – who was also to marry one of the officers – their French prisoner of war, Pierre, and the Polish maid Towka. Pierre and Towka were in love. They left the next day with Brigitte's mare Amica hitched to their dogcart, her young foal running by her side. With them were five other valuable Trakehner mares, including Arkade and Salamanca, pulling two wagons. One was driven by Pierre, who was a wine grower from the Bordeaux area and prisoner of war, and the other by Janek and Staszek, aged around 19 and 16 respectively. They were the young sons of a Polish couple who worked in the Pflaumbaums' dairy and who had begged Brigitte to take them with her to safety. The couple spent a two-week honeymoon on the estate of one of Heinz's fellow-officers at Bargensdorf in Brandenburg, and then Brigitte rejoined her family in their temporary lodgings at Georgental, near Insterburg, while her husband returned to the front.

By mid-October the front ran through Weedern, where the *Volkssturm* had dug two big anti-tank ditches. But the von Zitzewitzes and all the people who lived on the estate were still forbidden to leave. Even preparations for a trek were banned and Nazi officials kept coming round to make sure they were not secretly getting ready to go. They were even forbidden to slaughter more than a certain number of animals in case they should be stocking up on meat for the journey.

Nevertheless Anna von Zitzewitz, using the experience of their trek during the First World War, had already secretly planned the route and the number of horses and wagons they would take. She had also discreetly warned the families to be ready 'in case' they might have to go and told each one which wagon to take – there would be four to a wagon – 'if' the army should want them out of the way. But she had to be extremely careful whom she spoke to, for there could be informers among them. She had the harvest brought in early and got carpenters to fix wooden bars to the back of the wagons so she could tie three or four younger horses to each when they set off. When the Nazis demanded to know what these were for she had to hastily invent an excuse. It was a new-fangled device, she blustered, to anchor ties to steady high loads of hay so they would not fall off. They seemed to believe her.

It was a tense, anxious time. The East Prussian autumn, always breathtaking, seemed more golden, the sky wider and bluer, the air clearer and the countryside more beautiful than ever before. The storks had lifted off, circled and flown away southwards, leaving people wistfully wondering if and when they would ever see them again.

Soon the rains would come and with it the mud, and then the snow. The long and bitterly cold winter that bred in the people, as in their horses, a special toughness and resilience and an austere, hardy nature, was not far away.

EHLERT HAD BEEN whittling down his herds in Trakehnen. A number of young mares had been sold off to private breeders, and the two-and-a-half-year-old colts had already been distributed among the various *Landgestüte*. Soldiers had taken away Göring's 30 young mares. Many old people of Trakehnen and mothers with small children had been evacuated to Saxony. So by mid-October Ehlert and Seyffert imagined that at least some of Trakehnen's horses and inhabitants were out of danger.

Nevertheless more than 3,000 people and over 800 breeding horses, as well as the heavy draught horses, cattle and sheep, still remained in the stud, its village and outer farms. The raids by Soviet aircraft intensified; the artillery fire grew even louder. At night the sky was lit up by the glow of burning towns, flares and searchlights. It was now only a question of days, perhaps even hours, before the Russians reached them. But as ever, every phone call begging for permission to leave was met with a firm 'no'.

Ehlert was beginning to despair of getting all his human and equine charges away safely. With practically all his staff away at the war or in the *Volkssturm*, all he had left to evacuate 800 horses were the few old grooms and the inexperienced young stable boys – and these were also needed to drive the wagons in which the inhabitants would flee.

Exasperated, he wrote to Seyffert: 'how … at this time of year and in the face of imminent danger, some 800 horses and foals are to be removed on foot and housed and fed inside the province is a complete mystery.'

CHAPTER 6

At last!

It was the night of 15 October 1944 and Ehlert was expecting the evacuation order to come at any moment. The night sky was again lit up by burning towns. Flares shot upwards and disappeared; searchlights scoured the sky. He made phone call after phone call, but in vain. Midnight had long since passed, but he was in no mood for sleep. Instead, he drove over to the most easterly farm, which was right among the defence lines and the most vulnerable of all. He wanted to make sure that all would be able to leave as fast and smoothly as possible. The *Stallmeister* there was the best he had, an old East Prussian, whose roots lay deep in the land and whose whole life had been dedicated to horses. Like many in Trakehnen, he could not believe that this could be the end: that they would never come back again. And like several, he had decided not to go. Nothing Ehlert could say would make him change his mind. As he finally left in the early hours of the morning they shook hands, for the last time.

Back in Trakehnen, a troop of young horses was being led across the stud grounds in the chill, pre-dawn darkness, when a great roar arose in the east, a roar that swelled to deafening thunder. It was the opening barrage of the Red Army's artillery in the Soviet invasion of East Prussia. The war was coming home to Germany.

Shells fell all around, sending up clouds of dirt and debris. Horses panicked, neighing and plunging about; the stud was thrown into chaos. The angry rattle of anti-aircraft fire arose, heralding the approach of roaring formations of heavy Soviet bombers. The ground shook as bombs fell on the runways of the nearby airfield and on Trakehnen station. The squadrons turned north-west and headed for Gumbinnen.

The sun rose but the sky remained dark from the dust and only a thin grey light filtered through. The Russians had taken Eydkuhnen on the border and were advancing, while the German army was moving back. The Russians had sent up a tethered balloon from which they were spotting for their artillery. Fierce fighting was going on all around. The stud was turned into an advanced dressing station for wounded soldiers.

Another phone call. Everyone in Trakehnen was waiting anxiously for the order to evacuate; none came. Yet another call: still nothing.

That night Ehlert had all the horses from the various outlying farms and paddocks gathered together in large herds in preparation for the trek. It was not easy to move the horses around in the darkness, nervous as they were after the explosions and noise. Particularly terrified were the 20 small foals among them.

At five in the morning of the following day, 17 October, the phone rang. It was the District Administrator's office. Trakehnen was to be completely cleared: of people, horses, farm and domestic animals – and of its furniture, equipment and other contents. And, after having been forbidden for months to make any preparations, they were told that it must all happen within three hours.

The word spread like wildfire, and Trakehnen exploded into a frenzy of chaotic activity. White-faced and terrified, people were packing wagons and harnessing carthorses amid ambulances and tracked vehicles, stable boys were darting around among army and *Volkssturm* units. Otto Fiege was ordered into the saddle and told to report to a chief groom. They were going to take the horses away on foot.

In the midst of the confusion, at about eight o'clock, Lilli saw Herr Kowahl, the chief coachman, bring the Trakehnen coach up to the door of the *Landstallmeister*'s house. Suitcases and bags with their most essential belongings were stuffed under the seats, on top of them went bedding and Lilli, while her mother and her little brother sat on top of this. They were handed a basket of bread rolls. The doors closed and they moved off, followed by a second coach bringing the cook, the two maids and Herr Kowahl's wife. Everyone knew that the unimaginable was happening: they were leaving Trakehnen for ever. Lilli looked at her grandfather standing at the door and prayed that she would see him again that evening, as had been arranged, at the *Landgestüt* at Georgenburg.

Ehlert was at last able to put into action the plans he had been mulling over for so long. He had had the horses divided into 10 herds of about 80 each. To each herd he now assigned three men, one old groom and two young stable boys: one to lead, one to ride alongside and one to bring up the rear. It was not nearly enough and in order to keep the horses together, he gave them strict instructions to travel at a brisk trot and without stopping. Their destination was 54 kilometres away, the *Landgestüt* at Georgenburg, where Martin Heling was making room for them.

One after another, at intervals, the herds were sent off. But the moment they left their paddocks and joined the main roads, they met an endless flood of people fleeing their homes and farms; mostly women, children and old people, military vehicles, artillery, soldiers retreating from the front, people on foot carrying heavy bundles, or aboard hay-wagons, with hand carts, horses, sheep and cows. It was through this mêlée that the *Stallmeister* had to thread their way, while the refugees for the most part stood aside, astonished at the sight of these superb, gleaming horses passing at a smart trot, unshod, their foals running bravely alongside.

The herds from the farms north of Trakehnen station took the route along the main east–west road towards Gumbinnen and Insterburg. As they approached Gumbinnen they were met by the stench of burning. The town had been virtually destroyed by the air raid and many buildings were still in flames or smouldering. Through the smoke-filled streets they streamed, past charred and ruined houses until, in the central, chaotically crowded square, under the statue of King Friedrich Wilhelm II – the town's founder, as well as Trakehnen's – a dun-coloured mare stumbled and fell. Horses, herd animals by nature, instinctively follow those leading them and a sudden disruption can throw them into confusion. Brought to an abrupt halt, those behind her started milling around, frightened and bewildered. At that moment a panzer unit suddenly started up its engines, and the horses, terrified by the racket, fled, heading back in the direction from which they had come. A young stable boy dashed after them at a gallop, overtook them and barred their way with his own horse.

Gradually, calm and order were restored and the journey continued. But shortly after Gumbinnen they ran into a police roadblock: the main Gumbinnen–Insterburg highway was barred to all civilian traffic. They had to find their way along packed secondary roads, nervous of what would happen next. They did not know whether the army or the Nazi authorities were expecting them, whether they would be allowed to continue further on. They were only too accustomed to arbitrary changes of orders; they knew that anything could happen. Then there was the constant threat of strafing from enemy planes, and the cloud of dust that rose high over each herd as it travelled along the dry country lanes betrayed the presence of something unusual for miles around.

Other herds took a more southerly route without incident, until they reached a bridge over the steep, fast-flowing river Angerapp near Kanthausen. The bridge had been bombed to bits; only the supports still rose out of the water. Work on a makeshift replacement would take many hours, the nearest bridge was many kilometres away and the detour would make the journey far too long. The *Stallmeister* in charge decided to look for a ford that the horses could cross. While they waited, the other escorts had their work cut out to keep together their 80 charges, which, probably assuming they had reached their destination, tried to roam around at will, as they had done in their large paddocks at home.

A relatively shallow stretch of water was found about a kilometre away. The short, stocky *Stallmeister* coaxed his horse down the bank and swam across. One by one at first, then in groups, the horses swam after him. They scrambled up the opposite bank and shortly rejoined the road they had left. On they trotted, through the East Prussian landscape in all its sunlit autumn glory, through bombed and burning villages, leaping over fallen beams and masonry until in one village a group of Trakehners, attracted by neighs and whinnies, suddenly broke away and trotted through the open gates of a farm and into a courtyard where a number of yearlings and foals were penned up, waiting to leave with a local trek. Once again precious time was lost while their guardians searched for the truants and brought them back to the herd.

Otto Fiege and his two companions were in charge of a herd of two-year-old mares. They too set off cross-country, taking secondary roads and at times crossing fields. At one bridge, which acted as a bottleneck, one mare impaled herself on an iron bar and died instantly. The rest arrived safely and were found accommodation in the stables at Zwion.

The last herd had left Trakehnen at 11.30 in the morning and despite all the setbacks and detours that had extended their route to over 60 kilometres, the last horse had reached Georgenburg by 6.30 in the evening.

They had lost only one horse. One herd had been strafed, but suffered no casualties. Scarcely a single horse or foal was lame. 'And thus the Trakehners passed Koch's test with flying colours,' Ehlert was to write later. He himself arrived at Georgenburg later that day in a state of shock. He could not know that this had only been the first, and easiest, of his trials.

FIGHTING WAS RAGING around Weedern. Still they were forbidden to leave and told not to worry, as the Russians would soon be beaten back. Suddenly the German troops were streaming back towards them, retreating rapidly. They were astonished to find the von Zitzewitzes and their estate families still there. 'Get out quickly!' they shouted. 'The Russians are only a kilometre away!' Anna von Zitzewitz phoned the Nazi Party district office for permission, but there was no reply. The Brownshirts had already fled.

THE TRAKEHNEN HORSES were safe, for the moment. Not so the humans. The staff from the main stud and the 12 eastern farms had managed to leave by midday, not – as had been planned – in a single, cohesive trek as they had done twice during the First World War, but almost every wagon making its own way separately to Georgenburg. Most of the remaining men had been drafted into the *Volkssturm* and the 126 wagons were driven by women, schoolchildren, old men and prisoners of war. The young Helmut Hufenbach found himself driving a closed carriage packed with women and children. The deadline of three hours had, as Ehlert had foreseen, proved totally unrealistic. Moreover the instructions to remove all the contents of the stud had been quite out of the question: they had neither the staff nor the time to load and remove it. Like the herds of horses, they too were directed by the traffic police onto jammed secondary roads, where many of the heavily-laden wagons got hopelessly stuck. The local party office was asked to send help and eventually the *Volkssturm*, among them the very men who could have been driving the wagons, arrived to help heave them out. Some of the oxen, which were pulling a number of wagons, became so exhausted that they were useless and the two tractors in the trek had to ply to and fro, pulling out the stranded carts.

Behind them Trakehnen lay deserted, except for one or two old people who preferred not to leave. The statue of Tempelhüter was boarded up, in the hope of protecting it from damage.

Progress was extremely slow, but at least they were heading westwards. Not so the staff and families of the four most westerly farms which came under the Gumbinnen administrative district. There the local Party boss had flatly forbidden anyone to leave under pain of severe punishment. Ehlert had defied these orders by letting the horses from these farms go. But when the families tried to leave they were forcibly stopped and turned back. Two nights later some of them tried to slip away on their own initiative and to their horror found themselves overtaken by Russian tanks. The women and children managed to flee on foot, leaving everything behind. One driver who tried to save his family's belongings was beaten to death by Nazis in front of his wife. Others too, including young boys, were killed. Only the next day, 20 October, as the Russians arrived, came the official order to leave.

Stallupönen was in flames. There was fighting everywhere. Major Helmuth Hacke of Mounted Regiment 41, which had been rushed to the area when the Russians broke through, noted down on 20 October: 'I am lying as brigade group leader in the ditch alongside the road from Trakehnen station to Stallupönen (Ebenrode) directly to the east of Stubbenhof. In the foreground Amalienhof farm is burning, some 5km north-north east Trakehnen, and other places in the area. Everything looks eerie and ghostly.'

CHAPTER 7

Last Christmas at home

Then suddenly all was quiet. The fighting stopped; the Russians pulled back a little, but retained a presence. The front now ran through Trakehnen itself; Soviet units were camped on the Rominten Heath just to the south-east. The Nazis might boast that the Red Army had been beaten back, but in fact the Russians were sitting out the muddy season, in which their advance would easily get bogged down, and waiting for frost to harden the ground, freeze the rivers over and bring clear visibility.

It was then that the East Prussians learned of the horrors sweeping the countryside. News of the terrible atrocities committed by Soviet troops in the village of Nemmersdorf, only about 15 kilometres from Trakehnen, was broadcast on the radio and spread like wildfire. The tales were so horrifying that some could not believe them at first, assuming it was Nazi propaganda. But soon enough locals who arrived on the scene and foreign observers confirmed them to be true. Almost the entire civilian population, unarmed men, women and children, had been massacred in cold blood, often where they stood, in the streets, in their homes and in the fields. Girls and women had been savagely raped and murdered; some were found crucified, nailed by the hands and feet, to wagons or church doors. The crimes of the SS and the Wehrmacht in the east, of which most people knew little or nothing, were beginning to be avenged.

The Lehmanns could well believe what had happened. Their farm at Beszedszen, 9 kilometres southwest of Trakehnen, had for several days been a field dressing station for the Wehrmacht. At 7.30 in the morning on 20 October 1944, they too had fled amid a hail of artillery shells, taking 20 of their beautiful Trakehners with them. Everyone in the dressing station had fled too, leaving the wounded that were unable to move. Half an hour later the Red Army had entered the farm and the nearby village. Some days later, after the Soviets withdrew, almost the entire population of the village was found massacred. The heads of the wounded soldiers in the dressing station had been hacked off with spades.

As November approached, the golden autumn gave way to rain and cold. In Georgenburg every room of Dr Heling's large residence was crammed with refugees, who were being provided with food by his wife and their Georgenburg colleagues. The Trakehnen treks, however, had split up and moved on. Dr Ehlert and his staff moved to the state stud farm at Labes in Pomerania, while the farming staff and their families, led by *Obersattelmeister* Kiaulehn, trekked to Preussisch Eylau, where they found accommodation in a number of villages in the area.

INCREDIBLY, Anna von Zitzewitz had succeeded in mobilising her huge estate trek of some 380 people and

280 horses in two hours. Soviet tanks already barred the route she had planned to take, so she had to improvise. They headed westwards, travelling close to the front to avoid jammed roads, with Anna going on ahead in a trap to arrange accommodation at farms on the way. For several days they were accompanied by police escorts to protect them from attacks by partisans operating in the Kaschubei region. After 17 days on the road, they reached her brother-in-law's large estate at Gross Gansen in Pomerania, where they stayed, as they had done in the First World War, expecting to return in due course as they had done before.

The von Sperber trek had reached their designated quarters at Schöndamerau, south of Braunsberg in the western part of East Prussia. They hoped to continue with the few horses they had to Barbara's family's estate at Nauendorf, but the stationmaster told them there were no carriages or wagons available. In the meantime Barbara's *Mamsell* – the name given an East Prussian housekeeper – had been sent back to Lenken to collect a few more belongings and some chickens and geese for the pot. Barbara took one of the chickens and, without a word, placed it on the stationmaster's desk. When he heard about it, her husband's staunch Prussian upbringing caused him to burst out: 'How dare you do such a thing! That is bribery!' But sure enough, soon afterwards they were told that wagons were available and, principles or no principles, they set off by train for Nauendorf.

THE HORSES from the Trakehnen hunting stables were

sold to the army and a number of others not needed for breeding were sold off privately. The rest were shipped by rail to studs at Graditz in Saxony and Neustadt, to Labes and to half a dozen private estates in Silesia. But these proved to be seriously overcrowded and finally arrangements were made to house 290 mares and foals at a military horse depot at Perlin in Mecklenburg, where Dr Ehlert and his staff set up their headquarters. There were many problems to begin with, but Ehlert doubtless must have believed that at last he had saved both his family and most of his beloved horses from the Russians.

BY NOW GEORGENBURG itself was only a few kilometres from the front and, like Ehlert before him, Heling was trying desperately to make arrangements with the Gauleiter's office to send away his stallions. All he got was the confidential advice from an otherwise sympathetic official: 'Don't ever say another word on the subject if you don't want to be stood up against a wall and shot.' Eventually he was able to send many stallions to Braunsberg, and he and his wife Anni followed them. They stayed with Anni's mother, Charlotte Ramsch, widow of a former Prussian district president, who had an estate at Rödelshofen, conveniently close to Braunsberg.

Christmas was surreal. There were the Christmas trees, the gifts and the Christmas songs, yet at the back of everyone's minds was the fear that they may never see another Christmas, at least not in their homes or the land in which they grew up. Memories of that Christmas lingered for years. For Johanna Sasse it was packing 28 parcels for the men of the estate who were away at the war, and the sight of their 60 Russian prisoners of war crossing their courtyard, carrying the lighted Christmas trees, cakes and cigarettes they had been given – in defiance of Party orders – and singing. The French prisoners of war put pictures of Marshal Petain, the still-popular former ruler of unoccupied Vichy France, on their Christmas trees.

As if East Prussians were not scared enough, Hitler's New Year's message, printed in the *Königsberger Allgemeine*, painted the situation in the most terrifying, lurid terms. 'The categorical command: to win!' it began, 'or else we will all be destroyed in the greatest catastrophe that Europe has seen since the migrations of peoples.' Germans were facing 'a pitiless battle for existence' against a gigantic conspiracy by the British, with their 'satanic mentality', and by 'international Jewry' to destroy them. For the war was nothing less than an 'an attempt by the English and Americans to destroy Europe and Germany through Bolshevism and to have the German people punished – that is, eradicated – by the Muscovite murderers,' it ranted.

Koch followed it up with a message of his own: 'it is truly a battle for our existence, for our lives and our future … the personal destiny of every single German is at stake.' Everyone had to obey instructions unconditionally and, he concluded unconvincingly, 'where East Prussians stand, the Bolsheviks shall not pass'.

In Georgental, where the Pflaumbaums had been evacuated and were living in extremely cramped accommodation, Brigitte's mother broke her foot. The loss of her home had been a severe trauma and she no longer wished to live. Her husband put her on a train to the seaside resort of Cranz, north of Königsberg, to go and stay with a cousin, in the hopes that she would recover in more congenial surroundings.

Heling, now based in Braunsberg, continued his work. During a tour of the province he visited the fortifications set up to keep the Russians back. They looked formidable enough, but they were manned not by regular troops, but by a couple of pathetic-looking *Volkssturm* units. He realised that the Party propaganda about the impregnability of the Heilsberg Triangle and predictions that the Russians would be beaten back were all fabrication. It was quite clear to him what fate would soon befall the rest of East Prussia.

On 11 January 1945 he received a letter from the Agriculture Ministry passing on an order from Koch to gather together all the sires that remained in East Prussia and put them out to stud, because Koch was planning to send all the farmers back home to their farms.

CHAPTER 8

'... shall reap the whirlwind'

'We have reached the land of Erich Koch, the governor of the Ukraine. One need say no more. The day of judgment has come!'

The Red Army had not only been building up massive forces for the final invasion and defeat of Germany, but its soldiers' newspaper, *Krasnaya Svesda*, had been firing up to white heat its soldiers' hatred and desire for revenge on the enemy who had massacred, raped and plundered in their land. 'It is not enough to drive the Germans west, the Germans must be driven into their graves!' the paper declared.

Throughout the war the Soviet press and the political commissars had been preaching hatred of the Germans and now the propaganda machine was working at full steam. Just as Hitler's forces had committed all kinds of barbarism, now Stalin's men were being allowed – indeed actively encouraged – to take revenge on all Germans, guilty and innocent, soldiers and civilians, women and children. Property and women were to be theirs by right. Leaflets rained down on their positions as they waited to invade, with the incendiary words of the poet Ilya Ehrenburg: 'Kill, Red Army soldier, kill! May the blond beast be yours. Kill the child in the womb! Kill! Kill! Kill!'

Marshal Georgy Konstantinovitch Zhukov, the commander-in-chief of the 1st Belorussian Front, did not speak of rape or plunder, he did not need to. His order of the day as the troops were poised to invade ran: 'The time has come to settle accounts with the German fascist scoundrels. Great and intense is our hatred. We have not forgotten our burned-out towns and villages. We remember our brothers and sisters, our mothers and fathers, our wives and children, who were tormented to death by the Germans. We will avenge those burned in those diabolical ovens, those suffocated in gas chambers, those who were shot and tortured. *We take revenge for everything.*'

Hardened and coarsened by years of fighting, hardships and often hunger, Red Army divisions were only too ready to finish off the loathed enemy on his own soil. And at six in the morning on 13 January 1945, its presence masked by fog and low cloud, its 3rd Belorussian front opened fire in the north with an earth-shaking bombardment of nearly 120,000 rounds. Six days later the 2nd Belorussian front swept up from Poland, entered East Prussia from the south, and headed rapidly for Neidenburg and Allenstein, the German army retreating before them.

With them was a young Russian artillery captain who shared with his comrades the intense exhilaration of the invasion. He later poured all his excitement and tension, fear and horror of it into verse.

Open up, you alien country
Wide open let your gates be thrown

For, approaching, see how boldly
Russia's battle-line rolls on!
Hillock, dip, small bridge and hillock
Halt! Check on the map. –We're there.
Dismount! The foul witch [Germany] *shall remember*
Our salvo in the wintry air!
How many years now we've been stalking
Walking nearer, crawling near…
'Bat-tery! Into the sky of Prussia –
Load! – Ready! Three rounds! – Fire!'
There were wickedly cheerful faces
Sixty of them, windburned, black.
Into your vehicles! Get Moving!
Into Europe now! Attack!

It was every man for himself. Sometimes the phone call to evacuate came, sometimes it didn't. Planes were roaring and diving overhead, shells exploding everywhere. With the Russians only a few kilometres away, sometimes even entering their villages, East Prussians fled. The party officials were the first to go, abandoning the people they had kept pinned down for too long. People ran about in panic, frantically throwing carpets, bedding, clothes and food onto their wagons. They grabbed pots, pans, tools, guns, and – most important – horse fodder, as much as they could take of it, as well as buckets for their water and spare horseshoes. The trek leaders, usually farmers or estate owners, had been urging people to take only absolute necessities, but many could not part with precious belongings and the carts were piled higher and higher. Peter Elxnat's father, who was a great connoisseur of firearms, buried some 40 guns in a carefully concealed spot.

Tanks rumbled ever nearer, cannons roared. Horses were being harnessed, often four to a wagon, with the driver either riding the left-hand rear horse, traditional style, or on the box. Those horses not needed for pulling were attached to the wagons or led by hand by riders on other horses. Many of the wagons were rumbling hay carts with iron-clad wooden wheels; others were more comfortable carts with rubber tyres. There were tractors (such cars as they had had long since been requisitioned), hunting traps – anything on wheels. In Sabloczyn Karl Sasse was horrified to see his estate workers preparing sleighs. 'What are you thinking of? As soon as the snow melts you will be stranded!' he yelled at them. Fortunately they saw the point. Johanna Sasse threw in her family's coat of arms. They took with them their Polish forced labourers, who were as anxious to flee as they were. They told their 60 Russian prisoners of war to help themselves to the food that was left, but they could not take them; they would have to make their own way. The Russians were terrified, for they could expect no mercy from their own comrades: they had been ordered to fight to the death and cooperation with the enemy was seen as betrayal. In desperation they set off westwards themselves.

It was bitterly cold. The snow lay so deep on the ground that it almost reached the branches of the trees. Everyone was muffled up to the eyes in clothes, shawls, furs and sheepskins, but still they froze. The great flight had begun.

A land beyond our understanding
Nothing's like what it is with us!
It's not like Poland is, or home is –
Their roofs aren't thatched, their barns are firm as
Mansions cut from solid timbers …
Tiles, tiles – and see the towers,
All the turrets and the spires,
And houses built of solid brick.
We'd not be sorry to have suchlike
Things like that are pretty good!
A highroad runs through every village:
Each village – on a real road!

Out of their farms and estates they drove, some in large treks, others a family at a time, their horses pulling their wagons, others lashed to the side or led on a leading rein from horseback, on to the country lanes and from the lanes to the roads, only to find them jammed almost to a standstill by hundreds and thousands of other refugees with their wagons, grey-green army vehicles going to and from the front, columns of prisoners of war. Main roads were reserved for army use, several bridges had been bombed.

And there it began: the long, long nightmare that lasted weeks, even months; creeping forward at a snail's pace on the ice and snow, gripped by fear, with the roar of the *Stalinorgel* rocket launchers, the tanks and cannon fire close behind them; and beside them, enemy planes overhead, diving low and strafing the columns with machine-gun fire. Days and nights ran into each other in a confused blur, punctuated by episodes that etched themselves on their exhausted minds.

The Boettchers had driven out of Georgental with only minutes to spare. Brigitte and her father drove in the light dogcart. Pierre was behind with his beloved Towka; Staszek and Janek brought up the rear. They found themselves at a crossroads; Soviet planes were attacking, dropping phosphorus bombs. Horses were panicking, screaming and bolting; wounded people lay everywhere. It was chaos …

Gerd Lehmann, his mother Gerda and sister Elfriede with their wagon and 16 breeding horses – the rest had already perished – were passing through the marketplace of Osterode. The square and the streets around were jammed with trek wagons and military vehicles. Russian tanks came roaring in, firing mercilessly and crushing everything that lay in their path. Vehicles could not move forwards or backwards; people were screaming and running. Frau Lehmann grabbed her children and they ran for their lives. When they returned they found that their wagon and their horses had been flattened under the tracks of the tanks …

Burn the houses down, my brothers!
Ah, look how it's taking hold!
The walls won't catch? – Well start the rafters!
Fire the rafters first, you dolt!
No point in driving on, -eh, fellows?
Unless we leave them some mementoes?
Without orders, as it takes us,
Here, there, everywhere, look – scores
of smoky-red, dark-gleaming fires!
Well, now we're getting our revenge, lads,

We've hit him good and hard, the foe!

The Elxnats were woken at three in the morning. Peter's father took his wife and mother to the station, where there were frantic scenes as people struggled to board the last trains. Many of the 69 people – workers and their dependents – attached to their farm went with them. He then dropped in on the head of the local farmers' organisation to hear the latest news, and was told that the Russians were already in Insterburg and they should leave as soon as possible. By midday they were packed and off with 15 Trakehners, among them their dark brown mare Schwindlerin and her half-sister Filiale, both pregnant. Twelve of them were hitched to their six carts and three foals ran alongside. Peter's father led the way; an old farm worker drove the second wagon and three schoolboys the third, fourth and fifth, while Peter brought up the rear.

They could see Soviet tanks on both sides, already ahead of them. Profiting from Peter's experience in the war, they headed into the thick forest where they knew the tanks would not follow. If young Peter Elxnat was afraid he would not admit it, either then or any time afterwards. Young Prussian men and soldiers were not supposed to know fear …

Everything flames. Locked in their burning
Cowsheds, how the cows are bellowing –
　　Ah, poor creatures
　　But you're not ours!
What's more we have ourselves to save …

For right and left, on either side
What serpents rush and dance and glide!
On either side roofs meet the skies
– made of fiery dust, of stars,
of embers, glimmerings and sparks
Which shower down on our bended necks.
In the school the fiery wind
Hunts hungrily among the books.

Soon they saw the first corpses by the wayside, the first of many: babies who, despite thick, warm wrappings had frozen to death in their mothers' arms; children; old people who had died of cold and exhaustion, sometimes covered with a cloth or a layer of snow – there had not been time for anything else; bodies strewn around wrecked wagons shot to pieces by planes or smashed by tanks; dead horses, their legs sticking up in the air …

Franz Scharffetter had telephoned the previous evening to the district farmers' union and asked if it were time to trek. He was told to go to bed: in two days' time the Russians would be thrown out of East Prussia. In the early hours of the following morning he was woken and instructed to leave. He woke his prisoners of war, fed the horses, packed and by early evening had left Kallwischken with eight wagons, some of them with 2,000 kg loads, drawn by 22 of his prized Trakehner mares. Among them was the tough, brown Italia, daughter of Ita, who had starred in horse shows. She, like most of the others, was in foal. With the Russians only 3 kilometres away as he left, he drove for 24 hours without stopping, not even to feed or water the horses.

Brigitte's mare Amica's foal was slipping and stumbling helplessly. The axle of Pierre's wagon broke. In the confusion as they tried to repair it, the foal was becoming a liability and Brigitte realised it would have to be destroyed. But she could not bring herself to do it. In desperation she gave the foal to some soldiers and asked them to shoot it, but first to wait until she had gone. Then, tears streaming down her face, she drove off so that neither she nor Amica could see it die …

Someone breaks into the Gasthaus
And pushes a grand piano out!
Unable to drag it through the door
He bangs the strings with an old spade
and utters a delighted roar,
'If you can't be had by the warrior
Staff and Supply won't get you either
You swine …'
Another lurches without a care,
Far gone in booze, it's pretty plain,
Taking a resounding bash
At the nearest windowpane.
'Once I've gone I won't be back.
China – shatter! Crystal – crack!'

Candlelight was dancing in the dining room of the Haedge-Medicus manor house at Logdau; the family, relatives, friends and neighbours were sitting down to supper. But this was no celebration: the electricity had failed, the sound of war was coming ever nearer and the atmosphere was deathly. Everyone was heartbroken to leave home and terrified that they might never reach safety. The Sasses and their estate families had trekked over from Sabloczyn and they were all about to leave together, not knowing whether they would be able to get away safely. Outside the estate's distillery lay 14,000 litres of pure alcohol, which they had been unable to deliver for lack of transport. The Russians would be glad of it.

Here on their land had been fought the first battle of Tannenberg in 1410, the battle that effectively marked the end of the Teutonic Knights and the beginning of a long period of Polish suzerainty. Here a Grand Master of the order, Ulrich von Jungingen, was buried. Here four Haedge brothers had fought in the second battle of Tannenberg in 1914, this time a German victory, and the huge, triumphalist memorial stood only 4 kilometres away. One of the brothers, Max, had spotted a valuable hunting dog running, lost and terrified, between the lines. He caught it, later made enquiries as to its owners, and was led to the estate owners, the Medicus family, who could trace their ancestry back to the Florentine Medicis. He married their only daughter, tacked her name on to his and took over the estate. Now he was away fighting with the Luftwaffe. Another brother, ordered to help in the terrible task of reburying the dead from the battle, lost his mind and was confined in an institution. Recently the family had been informed he had died of pneumonia. They suspected, but never knew for sure, that he had been eliminated by the Nazis with others considered 'unworthy of life'.

For generations this place had been steeped in

Prussian and family history. As their great trek pulled out of the estate and on to the road they knew they were leaving forever. Karl Sasse, shattered by the loss of the estate that had meant so much to him, fell into a depression from which he never recovered.

And through the fires, the smoke, the soot,
The Conquerors of Europe swarm,
Russians scurrying everywhere.
In their trucks they stuff the loot.
Vacuum cleaners, wine and candles,
Skirts and picture-frames and pipes,
Brooches, medallions, blouses, buckles,
Typewriters (not with Russian type)
Rings of sausages, and cheese,
Small domestic ware and veils,
Combs and forks and wineglasses,
Samplers and shoes and scales …

Brigitte Boettcher, now alone in her dogcart, had reached the bridge over the river Pregel at Norkitten. Behind her were Pierre and Towka. Brigitte's father and the rest of their trek were far ahead. The treks were forced onto the right side of the road and had to wait while endless columns of military vehicles, tanks and soldiers streamed over the bridge. Amica, her beautiful five-year-old Trakehner mare, waited patiently. Amica had been given to Brigitte by her father when she was only a few months old. Brigitte had brought her up, broken and driven her in and looked after her lovingly. It was often lonely on their farm, especially in winter, and it was good to have a lovely creature to look after. She called her Amica – 'friend' – and Amica would follow her around the farm like a dog.

Hour upon hour passed, the noise of the *Stalinorgel* rocket launchers grew louder, and fear and tension mounted among the refugees. Along the endless line people were praying, others cursing, some were screaming, others weeping. As they passed Brigitte and the others a couple of soldiers bellowed to them 'What are you waiting for? The Russians will be here any minute. Leave everything and get yourselves to safety on foot!'

Leave her beloved mare? And her last belongings? Impossible! But what should she do? She had to get away, especially since she had not only herself to think of. She had recently discovered that she was expecting a baby. Suddenly on the left side of the road the long line of tanks ended and a horse-drawn unit appeared. Would anyone notice if she slipped in between the vehicles? She called to Pierre to follow her; they would break in to the column. But Pierre refused.

'I have order, I stay here.'

'Towka, come!' Brigitte screamed.

'No, I stay with Pierre!'

Exasperated, Brigitte touched Amica lightly with her whip and the mare set off at a brisk trot between army horses and wagons. They crossed the bridge and were off and away, with Staszek and Janek behind them, ignoring the shouts of the soldiers who were directing the traffic.

Shortly afterwards, as the soldiers had warned, the long queue of refugees waiting to cross the bridge was captured by the Russians. She never saw or heard of either Pierre or Towka again.

AMONG THOSE WAITING at the bridge was also part of the Georgenburg staff trek. A couple of Russian soldiers tried to seize the horses that were harnessed to one of their wagons. Enraged, an old Trakehnen official called Jucknat, who had been driving the wagon in front – a horse-drawn caravan with old women and children – intervened, shouting and threatening the armed soldiers with his only weapon – a stick. Taken aback, the soldiers desisted. But the Trakehnen trek was dispersed and the families had to try and make their way to the west as best they could, alone or in small groups.

Zweiundzwanzig, Höringstrasse.
It's not been burned, just looted, rifled.
A moaning, by the walls half-muffled:
The mother's wounded, still alive.
The little daughter's on the mattress,
Dead. How many have been on it?
A platoon? A company, perhaps?
The girl's been turned into a woman,
A woman turned into a corpse.
It's all come down to simple phrases:
Do not forget! Do not forgive!
Blood for blood! – *A tooth for a tooth!*
The mother begs, 'Töte mich, Soldat' [Kill me, soldier]

At another crossing, some 30 kilometres from Königsberg, a soldier controlling traffic directed Peter Elxnat's father and their second two wagons along one road. But the fourth wagon in the trek was stopped and directed with the others down another road. Peter, at the rear, could see the trek was being broken up, so he stopped the two other wagons in front and went on foot to find his father. He returned to find that the Russians had reached the spot and seized their three wagons and six horses. The drivers and passengers had fled. Gone forever were all Elxnat's personal belongings, documents and papers.

Around the same time, at a different spot, Elxnat's brother-in-law, Franz Girod, was captured by the Russians and compelled, with three or four other Germans, to drive some 1,000 head of cattle in the direction of Moscow. They set off, only to meet their end somewhere in the Soviet Union.

The Lehmanns had lost all their possessions, but friends had made room for them on their own wagon. They had managed to leave Osterode and were moving with the long stream of refugees slowly westwards from Liebesmuehl towards Saalfeld, when Soviet tanks roared into view and opened fire on the treks. Once again the Lehmanns ran for their lives and hid in a clump of bushes. When all was quiet and they ventured back to the road, they saw Soviet soldiers with machine guns lining refugees up on the side of the road and shooting them in cold blood. They fled in the opposite direction and managed to escape the massacre; but they were now at the mercy of the Russians …

THE EVENING after her escape at the bridge, Brigitte fetched up at a big farm, where many soldiers and refugees had found shelter for the night. She found a stable for Amica, fed her and went to find somewhere to sleep in one of the crowded rooms of the big house. Dog tired, she fell asleep, despite the din of artillery fire.

When she awoke the next morning, it was deathly quiet. She went out into the farmyard and stood here in absolute horror. It was completely deserted – and all the stable doors were open. The stable where she had left Amica the evening before was empty.

She was all alone: far from her father and sister who were at least a day's journey ahead of her, far from her husband who was somewhere at the front, and now her horse was gone!

She found someone who told her that since the enemy was approaching they had driven all the cattle and horses out on to the fields so they could feed on the haystacks there, and not starve abandoned in the stables. In desperation she went to her dogcart, which she had parked in a far corner of the yard. And there, in the corner, was Amica, all on her own! Brigitte could hardly believe that she had not left with the other horses, as any other horse would naturally do, but waited alone by the dogcart. Overjoyed, she harnessed her to the cart and they tore out of the farmyard, setting off again westwards, once again with only minutes to spare …

THE LEHMANNS were captured by the Russians, briefly interned and then released. They found themselves working on farms that had belonged to Germans but been handed over to Poles. At first they worked in a cattle shed, looking after cows. Later Gerd's mother and Elfriede found work in a mill run by Russians. They lived through weeks of terror, for Russian soldiers would frequently appear without warning and start gunning people down for no reason. They saw many people being shot, many others taken away and deported, presumably to the Soviet Union.

One day it looked as though their turn had come. They were rounded up in a farmyard by Russian soldiers with some 50 or 60 other people and told they were going to be taken to a place where they would be given new identity documents. The Lehmanns knew what this meant. Suddenly a Polish man appeared on the scene and Gerd realised he knew him – he had worked in the saddler's shop in his hometown of Budszedszen. The Pole saw him and asked what he was doing there, and whether there was anyone with him. Gerd explained that he was with his sister and mother. The Pole said something to the Soviet officer, who told the Lehmanns they could stay where they were. The rest of the Germans were taken away, never to return.

And … Cossacks go from carriage to carriage
Sabres ring and rifles thud.
'O-u-t!' And down the platform
In furcoats, hats and boots they herd -
'Leave your things!' they drive the helpless
Terrified civilians now
On foot to the collection depot
Across the town through rosy snow.
On the way they start selecting
Those they feel they want to spend a
Hot five minutes with in a doorway
Or any corner that comes handy.

Once again the Trakehnen staff were desperate to flee. Many had spent the winter months in Preussisch Eylau under the supervision of *Obersattelmeister* Kiaulehn, in the presumed safety of the western part of East Prussia. But now once again the Russians were only a few kilometres away and again they were forbidden to go. Except now the staff knew precisely what danger they faced and discipline was breaking down. Hufenbach and a group of other stable boys told Kiaulehn flatly that if he did not let them hitch the horses to the wagons and drive the families away, they would each grab a horse and a saddle and make off on his own.

Kiaulehn was not able to give the order and went off to the Nazi Party district office to get permission to go. He returned with it at one in the morning and that very night the trek set off through the deep snow. The staff and families had with them only the clothes on their backs and a sack with a minimum of belongings, but Kiaulehn joined in the procession with a box-wagon loaded down with his own property. The wagon kept getting stuck and holding up the trek, while the others had to pull it out. When they were able to stop for a rest, Hufenbach, furious, told Kiaulehn that if all the others were only allowed to take a sack each he did not need a whole wagonful of belongings. If he insisted on taking it he was not to stay with the trek. Kiaulehn refused to give up his box wagon and was left behind.

BY NO MEANS all the Soviet soldiers raped, murdered, plundered or set buildings on fire. Some officers tried to keep order and protect remaining Germans. They were appalled at the butchery and the senseless destruction of farms and towns, which they knew would soon belong to Russia. One such man was a Ukrainian propaganda officer by the name of Lev Kopelev. He spoke German and could see the individual humans and their suffering, rather than just hated enemy. With his pistol drawn he stopped drunken troops from raping girls and saved a number of Germans' lives. His compassion cost him nearly 10 years in prison camps.

For the young officer-poet who commanded the battery, the campaign only lasted three weeks. Somewhere near the Baltic, in an East Prussian manor house that had been taken over by the Red Army as a headquarters, Captain Aleksandr Solzhenitsyn was arrested. The censors had found critical comments about Stalin, even though he had used pseudonyms, in his letters to a former schoolmate. He was taken away by the secret police and later sentenced to eight years in the Gulag. There, struggling to come to terms with the right and wrong of it all, without writing materials, he composed this epic poem in his head and committed it to memory. He called it *Prussian Nights*.

CHAPTER 9

No way out but the Haff

The Boettchers, listening in secretly, heard it on Radio Beromünster, the free Swiss radio station, and froze with shock. Martin Heling and Hermann-Wilhelm von Warburg were told by railway officials at Braunsberg station, where a special train was supposed to take 75 Georgenburger sires from Braunsberg to safety. Thousands heard it to their horror as rumours or tips from soldiers, before it was finally announced on German radio.

The Red Army, pushing up from Warsaw, had reached the town of Elbing to the west. East Prussia was now surrounded by the enemy and their way to the west was cut off. Or almost.

'There's nothing for it but to go over the Haff,' declared Vera, Brigitte's sister. All agreed. If they drowned, they drowned: far better than being captured by the Russians.

The Frische Haff was the more westerly of two long freshwater lagoons that lay along the Baltic coast of East Prussia, and was separated from the sea by a long, very narrow strip of land called the Frische Nehrung. In winter it usually froze over and the ice provided short cuts between the little villages on the Nehrung and the mainland. Now it was frozen solid and covered with snow, a flat expanse of whiteness with the dunes and woods of the Nehrung barely visible between four and 12 kilometres away. The Wehrmacht was fighting desperately to keep the Russians from reaching it. If they could cross the Haff, they could trek westwards along the Nehrung, pass north of Elbing, where the Russians had not yet penetrated, and reach Danzig and points to the west.

But running along the ice, a black strip in the whiteness, was a channel cut by naval icebreakers to allow newly-built submarines from Elbing to reach the Pillau at the eastern end of the Haff and the passage to the open sea. It was also used to bring weapons and supplies to the army at Elbing. This black strip lay between some hundreds of thousands of refugees, thousands of horses and their chances of reaching safety.

In Braunsberg Martin Heling contacted the deputy District Administrator, a friend of his, who told him in confidence – just as much else that would decide the lives and deaths of countless people was kept confidential – that a wooden bridge was being built over the channel. He and von Warburg quickly made plans. Once again Trakehners would have to escape on foot. And on 27 January 1945, with the Russians only 5 kilometres away, 100 Braunsberger and Georgenberger sires streamed out of the Braunsberg stud. Led by von Warburg and what few grooms he could still muster, they wound their way to the fishing village of Alt Passarge and, in an icy blizzard, across the Haff to Narmeln. Their destination was the study at Redefin, in western Mecklenburg.

Another 140 stallions remained for the moment in Braunsberg, as von Warburg did not have enough staff to accompany them. Instead they were placed in the care of an army veterinary unit.

FRANZ SCHARFFETTER and his trek were also at Braunsberg, where they had paused for a couple of days. He had sent six of his 22 horses back in the direction of Kallwischken with his Russian workers when Koch's office had started telling people to return. He too set off across the Haff, probably anxious about his wife, his son Hans-Joachim and two other children who were staying in Liebstadt, some 50 kilometres to the south. But they had been woken in the middle of the previous night with the warning that the Russians were approaching Elbing. They hastily set off with a friend in a tractor-driven wagon, passed Elbing the next morning and headed westwards just a few hours before East Prussia was cut off.

The Braunsberg staff had formed a trek and the Helings had set off in advance to arrange quarters for them. They travelled in an open hunting trap pulled by two black Trakehner stallions, with Heling's coachman Gallinat on the box. Reluctantly, they left Anni's mother behind: as a good lady of the manor, Frau Ramsch could not bring herself to leave her estate workers. It was around 20 degrees below zero, driving snow lashed their faces and cut visibility down to a few metres but, they were able to console themselves, at least it kept enemy bombers away. At Alt-Passarge they ventured down on to the Haff and when they came to the bridge he and Anni walked one on each side, and holding the trembling horses by the bridles, coaxed them over the swaying logs. As they headed over the ice towards Narmeln they were devastated at the heart-rending sight of terrified refugees struggling across on foot, often with tiny children, and mostly completely inadequately clothed and shod for the bitter cold and snow. They took on board a young mother, a teacher, who was towing a small child behind her on a toy sledge, but there was no room for anyone else. Even though their hunting trap was loaded high with fodder and hung about with feeding buckets they were still subjected to insults from the unfortunate pedestrians: 'Here comes the Baron!'

Finally they reached the Nehrung, only to find that their nightmare had hardly begun. The narrow road along the dunes was now the only route to the west and both pedestrians and horse-drawn wagons were constantly being forced off the road by military vehicles and endless columns of prisoners of war into the deep snow and soft sand on either side. After 12 hours of slowly dragging themselves forwards – it was by now night – they reached the village of Stutthof at the end of the Nehrung, ran into a deep snowdrift and got stuck. Try as they might, the stallions, up to their bellies in snow and exhausted after the hard 75-kilometre journey, were unable to pull it out. There was nothing left but to unharness the horses, which Gallinat led to the nearest farmstead in search of shelter. The farmstead turned out also to be an inn, swarming with soldiers, and Anni and their passenger went to try and keep warm while Heling stayed to guard the trap, which was repeatedly being bumped by ruthless lorry-drivers. He heard a familiar swearing loudly and as it drew closer he realised it was none other than Franz Scharffetter leading his Kallwischken trek, composed mostly of women. Between them the two men and the Kallwischken women dug and pulled the trap free and pushed it to the farmstead. Heling had to spend the rest of the night in a freezing cold barn with his pistol drawn, protecting his two black Trakehner stallions from marauding soldiers.

The next day it was snowing heavily and Heling set out in search of quarters for the Braunsberger trek. He found a disused factory where they could at least find shelter, if not much comfort. During his search, he ran into an officer of the Mounted SS whom he knew and who told him that he had been sent to evacuate the inmates of the nearby concentration camp. Heling was astonished: like many other East Prussians, he had no idea that there was a concentration camp in the region. He would not have seen the inmates, mostly women, mostly Jews, leaving the typhoid and smallpox-ridden hell that was the camp, 1,000 to 1,500 at a time, weak, starving, often shoeless, and insufficiently clothed. Their 'evacuation' meant being driven by their guards westwards on death marches through the ice and snow, leaving a trail of blood and corpses in their wake. He was later to meet up with such victims of the Nazi regime and still not realise quite what they had been through; but that was still to come.

NIGHTMARE though their crossing was, the Helings, the Braunsberger and Kallwischken treks and others who managed to get across early, were lucky. For after a few days the cold spell broke, a thaw set in and the ice began to melt.

By then there were half a dozen routes across the Haff. Troops had been testing passages across the ice and marking them out with fir trees or lanterns. More logs were placed over the channel and dangerous parts of the ice. The routes crossed the ice diagonally, so that the way was longer, around 20 kilometres. Soldiers, struggling to regulate the traffic on the shore, made refugees throw out all but absolutely essential baggage to lighten the wagons and the roadside was strewn with jettisoned belongings. As they approached the ice, the wagon drivers were obliged to take on board as many pedestrians as possible.

The ice by the shore was the first to go soft and the soldiers tried to make wagon-drivers keep a distance of 50 metres from the wagon ahead. But with the din of the bombing and the cannon coming ever closer, many panicked and made a dash for the ice all at once. Peter Elxnat watched in horror as the ice broke, wagons sank and the occupants and horses, screaming helplessly, were drowned.

The Elxnat trek, which had been joined by some neighbours from their village, moved westwards, keeping close to the shore on the first day. On the second, taking advantage of a blizzard that kept Soviet planes away, they struck out diagonally across the Haff, following one of the routes. When visibility became too poor to see the fir trees they simply followed the line of corpses, humans and horses and wrecked vehicles, across the frozen waste. Somewhere out on the Haff, tragedy struck their neighbour's trek: an elderly woman died of cold. She was rolled in a carpet and put on the back of the wagon.

Some drivers had brought metal spikes with them that could be attached to the horses' hooves to give them a better grip. But other horses, with their iron shoes, were constantly slipping, crashing onto the ice, picking themselves up again and falling again. Often horses and people were wading knee deep in icy water, unable to see where next to put their feet. The ice was cracking up and holes were everywhere. Refugees in closed carriages got out and walked alongside, or travelled with the doors wide open. If the vehicle capsized or sank, they did not want to be trapped inside. All the time they were flanked by people fleeing on foot, desperate and wounded, without an arm, an eye, on crutches, children in pushchairs and sledges.

After three days on the ice the Elxnats finally reached the Nehrung and, like thousands of others, were dismayed to find that there was no food available anywhere for man or beast. The ravenous horses took to eating the thatch from the roofs of houses as they passed.

As the visibility cleared, Soviet aircraft roared over during the daytime, bombing the defenceless refugees clearly visible against the whiteness of the ice and snow. Fountains of water rose high in the air where the bombs fell, making large craters in the ice. Some thought they could see vehicles in the distance, apparently crossing the ice. But on closer study they were not moving; they were burned-out Wehrmacht vehicles that had been bombed. Corpses lay strewn around.

Brigitte and her trek set out at night. It was impossible to see whether the ice ahead of them was safe or not. Hour after hour they crept forward, walking gingerly alongside the horses, not knowing if their next step would be their last, but trusting in the animals' powerful instincts. To the left and right of her were dead bodies, of people and horses, and the wreckage of wagons.

ON 2 FEBRUARY 1945, the head of the horse clinic in Königsberg, army veterinary officer Dr Ernst Arnold, received the order to take some 100 stallions from Braunsberg to the stud at Labes. His route was dictated to him in precise detail and led through Elbing, on the assumption that the Germans would have retaken the town. Fully aware that this was highly unlikely, and that they would therefore never reach their destination, Dr Arnold spent a night in difficult negotiations with his superiors until he finally wrung from them a written order stipulating 'that the officer in charge may take another route if the one he was instructed to take seems inadvisable'.

The next day Arnold, with the help of a respected local breeder, selected 103 of the best Trakehner stallions in Braunsberg and 11 pedigree carthorses that were also housed there. With 90 men from the hospital staff and 75 Russian prisoner-of-war volunteers riding and leading the horses and with fodder and food ration wagons, he set off westwards towards Frauenburg on the Haff. On the way they ran into a Russian bomb attack, which threw the horses into confusion and forced the column to halt until things had quietened down. There were no victims and Arnold was relieved to see that his Russians were excellent horsemen.

Fortunately the Haff had frozen over again, the temperature was back down to minus 20 degrees. The ice was like glass. They had been joined by more than 360 army mounts ridden or led by other soldiers. Blacksmiths who had been posted by the shore for that purpose took the iron shoes off the horses. Defying orders by Koch to cross by daylight and thus risk innumerable losses, they ventured on to the ice in the late afternoon and headed for the Nehrung, picking up civilians on the way who had been injured or had their wagons destroyed by Soviet aircraft. One carthorse fell, broke a leg and had to be shot.

The sires, after a long period of inactivity and a high-energy diet in Braunsberg, were extremely frisky and once on the crowded Nehrung road, repeatedly caused havoc among the columns of refugees. Arnold let the quieter military horses continue towards Stutthof, while he headed northwards with his sires over the dunes to the Baltic shore and marched along the beach. It was, he recalled later 'a ghastly, yet beautiful sight, as the long line of horses and riders crossed the dunes, lit up brightly by the glare from the little town of Tolkemit that was burning about 12 kilometres away'.

WITH THE NEHRUNG behind them, the refugees' journey became somewhat easier. They were back on hard roads; food and fodder were easier to come by. But ahead of them was the river Nogat and further on, the broad Vistula: behind and to the south of them, their cannon only too audible and the burning towns visible, were the Russians. Here again thousands upon thousands of refugees were held up at the few bridges, terrified they would not be able to cross in time, while the army insisted on priority for its troops and weapons. The Sasses' trek experienced anxious hours as they picked their way along a slippery, ice-covered dam in the Vistula delta, walking beside their horses and holding their heads for fear they would slip and bring everything crashing down the steep banks. Suddenly they were confronted with a dead horse in their path. Horses will not pass close to a dead one of their kind and sure enough, their own horses stopped and refused to budge an inch. For what seemed an eternity, their trek and many others behind them were stuck, unable to move forward or back. Eventually a group of *Volkssturm* men came to the rescue and with tremendous effort shifted the dead weight of the horse off the track and down the bank, so they could move on.

In Danzig the Nazis still had total control. Brigitte saw bodies hanging from lampposts – deserters, perhaps, or locals who had tried to flee. Soon they ran into a *Greifkommando*, a press gang of brownshirted Nazi thugs, who seized Janek and tried to drag him off to help build fortifications. There was a wild argument; Brigitte tried to grab him back and Staszek was in tears. There was a tug-of-war and the Nazis carted Janek off. Staszek, who did not want to be separated from his brother, went too. Brigitte never knew what became of them.

Part of the Trakehnen staff trek reached the Danzig area, but there their horses were requisitioned by the army. Stuck without transport, most of them had to settle in the area and never reached the west.

In Stutthof Heling had managed to exchange his hunting trap for a sleigh and as soon as the snow stopped, on 1 February, they set off westwards again. By good fortune they were able to cross the Vistula quickly and soon reached Danzig where, however, it was raining, the snow was melting fast and the sleigh was running into difficulties. Heling parked in a quiet, snowy side street while he went to try and get maps and exchange the sleigh for another vehicle. When he returned he found, standing near his sleigh, a Georgenburg carriage and in it the head of the Georgenburg cashier's office, a man called Baller. Part of the Georgenburg trek, including the office staff and contents, had taken a different route westwards and fetched up at the *Landgestüt* of Preussisch Stargard on the western side of the Vistula. But since the Russians were pushing up from the south, the *Landstallmeister* there had sent the entire stud up to Danzig, where the local army veterinary department had arranged transport for them by rail to the state stud farm at Labes. They were due to leave the next morning! Heling could hardly believe the good news, nor the amazing coincidence that Baller should have been in the same street at the same time as they.

The next morning Heling and his staff settled down together as best they could on straw in the horse-wagons for a four-day journey in the direction of Labes. It was hardly a pleasant journey. Armed men, probably deserters, tried to force their way onto the wagons, threatening to shoot if they were denied entry. But the

Georgenburgers were in a happy mood, delighted to be together again and relieved to be heading for safety, and gladly shared such food as they had with each other. Heling was to remark later how nice everyone was to each other in those difficult days. But 'it was above all during the four-day journey in railway wagons that we saw for the first time quite how loyally, how affectionately, how decently and how tactfully everyone, without exception, behaved, particularly in view of certain embarrassing situations made unavoidable by such a long journey.

'Certainly,' he added, 'to be absolutely objective, in the large Georgenburg/Zwion community there were some types who gave themselves airs as the appointed guardians of the "ideology" and there were some rather murky figures. But most were upright, well-mannered and faithful.'

By good fortune the train stopped at the station of Köslin, where Heling's sister lived. On impulse, he handed over the responsibility for the trek to three senior stud officials and he and his wife got out. They were desperate to know what had become of their 15-year-old son Dietrich. They had not seen or heard of him since a few days before their own departure when, in the hopes that he, at least, would not fall into the hands of the Russians, they had sent him off on foot across the Frische Haff in the company of an uncle. To their great joy they found him safe and sound, and although it was still in the early hours of the morning, he threw himself in his nightshirt into the arms of his overjoyed mother. Dietrich and his uncle had reached the Nehrung safely, been taken on board a naval vessel and shipped to Neufahrwasser near Danzig. After they boarded a train westwards, terrible scenes of panic and destruction broke out – Soviet bombers were blasting the station. They were unhurt but travelled the rest of the way to Köslin in an icy train with all its windows and doors smashed.

CHAPTER 10

The end of Trakehnen

Before the Soviet invasion West Prussia, Silesia, Pomerania and Mecklenburg to their west had been considered by East Prussians to be well out of reach of the Russians and therefore safe. A number of children had been sent there, and the East Prussian Studbook Society had evacuated many privately owned young horses to be looked after by breeders there. The Sasses had sent clothing to friends in the Lausitz area, the Dohnas had sent their four children to their grandmother in Bad Muskau by the river Neisse and two wagonloads of clothing, linen and furs to a friend on the western side of the Vistula river in case they had to flee without any belongings. Many evacuees were staying there, waiting until it became possible to return home again. In October 1944 the von Zitzewitz trek from Weedern had taken refuge on the estate of Anna's brother-in-law at Gross-Gansen, near Stolp, just as it had done in the First World War. It was during that first stay, some three decades earlier, that their great stallion Bulgarenzar was born. He was later sold to Trakehnen and become one of its most famous sires. No future great stallion was born there in the winter of 1944, however.

Stalin was out to grab as much of Germany as he

could, and he was determined that the Russians should reach Berlin first, ahead of his western allies. His armies were pushing relentlessly westwards and northwards, seizing the regions along the Baltic coast piece by piece and driving towards the heart of Germany. By now millions of Germans were fleeing and many headed for coastal ports and harbours, where the navy had mounted a massive marine rescue operation – reminiscent of Dunkirk – to bring them to safety.

At Gross-Gansen Anna von Zitzewitz realised they would have to move on. Although the Weedern trek had reached there safely, the trek from her estate at Kleszowen, which had set off a day later, had fallen into the hands of the Russians and all 200-odd people and a large number of brood mares had perished. Anna knew what they risked if they stayed. Nevertheless, much as she tried to persuade them, her estate workers and office staff refused to go. Many of the women were anxious about their menfolk in the *Volkssturm* back at home, and they wanted to return in time for the spring ploughing and sowing on their patches of land, otherwise there would be no produce that year. More powerful still, the thought of setting out for an uncertain destination in raging snowstorms and bitter cold, with the danger of being shot to pieces by enemy aircraft or mown down by tanks, was just too much for them to face. So with her two children – 13-year-old Eberhard and 12-year-old Erdmute – and another family, Anna set off again, taking 74 of her best horses with her. Some of the horses were harnessed two or four-in-hand, the rest were ridden or led by themselves and their French and Belgian prisoners of war. The rest of her horses she reluctantly had to leave behind in Pomerania.

The first trek in October had been relatively easy. This time it was a struggle for survival. They spent nights camping hidden in the frozen woods; in the morning the horses would be covered with hoar frost. By day Soviet planes roared low overhead, firing at the treks. And when they stumbled on American units advancing from the west they were scarcely safer: as they hid in a forest, an American tank suddenly appeared and one of three young mares that Erdmute was leading by hand was shot dead. Finally they reached the Elbe. Like thousands of other exhausted and desperate refugees, they were sure that once across, they would have little to fear. But they were too late, the border between the Soviet and western zones had already been drawn and sealed off. They were forbidden to cross.

JOHANNA SASSE, with her husband, mother, sisters and their trek, had fetched up on the estate of a Herr von Bülow in Pomerania. Like all such places along the escape routes, it was crammed with refugees. It was a dreadful moment. Once again the enemy was approaching; once again there was a ban on leaving. They were terrified to make a move. Herr von Bülow had found his neighbour shot by the SS and hanging from a tree: he had been preparing to flee. It was a terrible warning.

One night Johanna was lying on the floor of a crowded room, unable to sleep, when the door opened and a tall, slim figure looked in and asked if there was space to lie down. Johanna made room and since neither of them felt like sleeping, they talked all night. The next morning when her husband woke up he stared at the stranger in astonishment.

'Herr Sasse!'

'Prince Dohna!'

The stranger was Alexander von Dohna-Schlobitten, who was leading his huge trek westwards and had lost his way while reconnoitring for the next stage of their journey. The two men had been in the same regiment.

Dohna invited the Sasse–Haedge-Medicus family and their trek to join his, which they gladly accepted. For him, as he wrote years later, 'it was a pleasant change to be able to talk at last with pretty young ladies about anything else except the trek, and to begin an amusing flirt with the youngest one.' For his new companions it may well have been their salvation.

Dohna, more than most people, could see through the lies and propaganda of the regime and knew that they must get as far west as possible, where the Americans and British would be. It was not easy to convince everyone, for many still believed blindly in the myth of the 'wonder weapons' that would put an end to the war. And the further they moved west, the more anxious his people became to return home as soon as possible to plough and sow the fields.

Dohna had realised that the fastest way was to trek by night, when the roads were clearer, and to sleep by day, when there was room in whatever accommodation they could find on the way. That way they also avoided being rammed by German tanks, shot at by enemy planes, or having their remaining menfolk seized by

Nazi press gangs and sent to the *Volkssturm*. He would ride ahead on his horse, Ollo, or in a light trap to gather information about which routes were open and to arrange accommodation. His name, his appearance – in a military fur greatcoat with a Russian fur hat – and the size of his trek carried considerable weight. During one such expedition a few days later, he learned that the ban on trekking was to be lifted in a few hours and he instructed everyone to prepare; they would leave that very night.

Again thousands upon thousands of desperate refugees were held up in endless queues at the few bridges, while the army insisted on priority for its troops and weapons. For three days and three nights, with temperatures plunging at times to minus 30 degrees centigrade, the Sasses and Dohnas waited at the Autobahn bridge over the Oder, south of Stettin, frozen to the marrow and terrified the Russians would reach them before they could cross.

Somewhere on those frozen white wastes, despite all its warm wrappings, a baby in their trek died. It was buried, like countless others, in the snow at the side of the road. There was time to pause only for a moment; they had to move on.

For much of the trek, Johanna Sasse had been riding one of her horses and leading a black Irish thoroughbred stallion, with the leading-rein wrapped around the fingers of her right hand. Her fingers froze stiff and she could no longer use them. A doctor diagnosed frostbite and said she would have to have her fingers amputated. Johanna objected, and by steadfastly dipping them alternately in hot and cold water she managed gradually to nurse them slowly back to life.

IN BERLIN the Agriculture Ministry in the Wilhelmstrasse was bombed out and Seyffert evacuated his offices, himself and his family to Neustadt on the Dosse. Neustadt consisted of a *Hauptgestüt*, a main state stud farm where the Brandenburger breed was developed, and a *Landgestüt*, a regional state stud farm where the Brandenburg stallions were kept. There, as in Berlin, Seyffert was at the centre of the web of operations, directing evacuations, battling for transport, negotiating with the Wehrmacht and the party authorities, and making financial arrangements. As the Red Army advanced westwards and northwards, the various German stud farms with their vast stables and facilities became stepping stones in the westward flight of the breed, from Trakehnen to Georgenburg, Georgenburg to Braunsberg, then Preussisch Stargard in West Prussia, Labes, then Redefin in Mecklenburg , Neustadt, Graditz and Moritzburg in Saxony. All the time he was in touch with the various *Landstallmeister* who reported to him from en route as best they could. Often the usual formal typed letters gave way to scribbled notes on exercise paper, long handwritten scrawls – particularly from Heling: postcards, telegrams and, if they were lucky, phone calls.

Seyffert was still associated with the SS's *Rasse- und Siedlungshauptamt* (Race and Settlement Office), which had become deeply involved in the ethnic cleansing and German colonisation of conquered countries. His exact role is unknown but probably still minor, although he had taken care to inform it of his change of address. At the same time he was very wrapped up in his efforts to save the Trakheners. Deep anxiety for his breeders and horses seeps through the Prussian formality of his official correspondence. As Marienwerder was about to be overrun and he was unable to reach *Landstallmeister* Hans Ehlers by phone, Seyffert had to write by registered mail informing him he had not been able to find any transport for the horses and added: 'I am extremely distressed not to be able to help you from here in your desperate situation.' He made the obligatory assurances of victory – he could never know who else would read the letter – but then urged Ehlers to get his own family and those of the staff out to safety as soon as possible. 'I beg you, no matter what happens, to keep a cool head … my thoughts are with you more than ever,' he wrote.

Ehlers managed to bring many of his horses on foot to Labes but there was little respite as the Soviet juggernaut rolled on. A month later Seyffert received a telegram from Labes dated 23 February 1945: 'EHLERS HEADED KÖSLIN AREA WITH SOME 70 STALLIONS DESTINATION SWINEMÜNDE.'

Ehlers managed to bring his horses almost to the Elbe when they were seized by the Russians; he himself escaped to the west. The *Landstallmeister* of Labes, Althaus, tried to escape with his stallions on foot, but they too were captured. Althaus was shot and fell dead from his saddle.

Altogether 115 Georgenburger stallions had been evacuated to Labes and before the Russians came Heling managed to ship 60 to Neustadt. Another five were out to stud. He put the remaining 60 in the care of his trusty chief groom, Balszuweit, and on 4 March they too set off in the direction of Neustadt. However, the following day they were surrounded by Soviet tanks and soldiers. Balszuweit was taken prisoner and the horses sent back to Labes, where their fate is unknown.

Meanwhile Heling and his wife Anni had reached Neustadt, where the Seyfferts were living. Their son Dietrich, who had arrived ahead of them, had made friends with the Seyfferts' two boys and was staying with them while his parents, for lack of accommodation in the Neustadt, had to lodge with friends in a nearby village. To their relief, Anni's mother, who had insisted on staying and trekking with her estate workers, reached them safely.

Heling had long since realised that the only hope of saving at least some remnants of the Trakehner breed and building it up again, lay to the west of the Elbe, the part of Germany which would be controlled by the British and Americans. But he dared not say so, for even then, in March 1945, with most of the country overrun, the propaganda machine was still promising a glorious victory and anyone who doubted it was punished, as ever, for defeatism. Fortunately, however, the East Prussians had more freedom to move around than local people and without letting his reasons be known, Heling managed to arrange for 30 Georgenburger stallions to be shipped to Celle. He also sent couriers – it would have been too dangerous to write or telephone – to other stud farms where his horses were being kept to try and arrange discreetly to send them to Celle on foot.

The *Landstallmeister* of Neustadt, Hans Güntzel, was friendly, welcoming and helpful to his displaced colleague, but he was also a diehard Nazi. When Heling cautiously advanced the possibility that he might make plans to evacuate Neustadt, Güntzel flatly rejected the idea. Güntzel had complete confidence in the Führer. He was entirely convinced that Hitler had 'wonder weapons' and that he would deploy them when the right moment came. He was to bitterly regret his blind faith.

April arrived and time was getting short. Heling pressed Seyffert to allow him to transfer his office and his stallions to Celle in Lower Saxony. Seyffert objected at first, arguing that the western Allies were likely to reach the Elbe before a trek from Neustadt could, and would bar them from crossing the river. But finally he relented, on condition that they went by train.

This was easier said than done. By that stage, in the chaos of war, with millions of refugees heading westwards, rolling stock was in desperately short supply. Besides, the only still functioning line westwards out of Neustadt went via Rathenow and did not belong to the state railways, which meant that they had a very limited number of wagons. But the stationmaster knew Heling from the time when he was *Landstallmeister* at Neustadt and declared that 'as a former cavalryman' he could not bring himself to prevent East Prussians reaching freedom in the west.

He managed to conjure up a few wagons and Heling had to be content to load up 12 of his stallions, his administrative staff, a few other Georgenburgers and the contents of his office. And so, on the evening of 6 April, hooked up to a train, they left Rathenow. The stationmaster predicted that it would be the last train he would send out of his station before the Russians came.

They arrived at Rathenow – and stopped. The stationmaster there refused flatly to send them on any further. After endless pleading he made Heling a vague promise 'as a former cavalryman' that if a train should arrive, he would disobey orders and stop it. And in fact, in the early hours of the morning, a western-bound SS hospital train arrived and was stopped at the signals. The SS doctors were very obliging. They regretted that they could not take the Georgenburgers to Celle but offered to take them at least to the station of Isenhagen-Hankensbüttel, from where a branch line led to Celle.

The Georgenburgers were hooked up and set off on a hair-raising journey westwards, during which the train was repeatedly strafed by enemy planes. Nevertheless, by 7 pm they were duly deposited unharmed just outside the station of Isenhagen-Hankensbüttel. The first thing Heling saw was a locomotive steaming up ready to pull out. He raced towards it and begged the railwaymen to take them too. They told him this was the last train to Celle and it already had more wagons than was permitted. But – Heling could hardly believe his ears – the stationmaster revealed he too was an 'old cavalryman'. And sure enough, he had the Georgenburgers hooked up to his last train and that night, to their immense relief, they pulled into the blacked-out station of Celle. They spent the rest of the night in the bachelor apartment of the Celle *Landstallmeister*, Korndorff, and at dawn the next day – 8 April – unloaded the stallions.

That afternoon Celle station was devastated by a British bomb attack. Theirs had been one of the last two trains to arrive in safety.

Among those who remained in Neustadt was Otto Fiege. After accompanying the two sires to Neustadt, Fiege had stayed on and continued his training to become a groom. A few days after the Georgenburgers left, he was working with an old groom near the Schloss. Between the buildings – on the left the sires' stables, on the right the stables for the draught horses – he could see the river Dosse flowing quietly through the nearby meadows. The peace was broken by his older companion, who remarked in a quiet voice, 'Oh, The Russians are coming!'

As if from nowhere, Russian soldiers galloped in. They opened the stables, took five of the best stallions out of their stalls and rode off on them, leaving their own smaller, rougher horses behind. It was too late now even to think of escape. They were surrounded and being closely watched.

On 2 May, Güntzel, in a gentlemanly manner, formally handed over the keys of the stud farm to the senior Soviet officer. He perhaps expected he would be treated with similar correctness. Instead he was given two hours to get out of the *Landstallmeister*'s residence. He was then stripped of all his possessions, arrested and interned in the Brandenburg transit camp, from which thousands were being deported to slave labour in the Soviet Union.

Two weeks later the staff at Neustadt could see something that seemed to be a commission of experts arriving. A red carpet was put out and one by one horses were paraded in front of them. Then the horses were loaded on to trains, amid indignant protests by the German staff, for no care was taken to put the foals with the right mares. A young foal separated from its mother was very likely to perish. Stallions were loaded together and not tied up – they feared that the high-spirited and rivalrous animals would tear each other apart. How many reached their destination, and in what condition, they never knew.

The *Hauptgestüt* filled up with tanks and lorries. In the stables of the *Landgestüt* where the horses had once stood were now cows, pigs and sheep, needed to feed the population of the Soviet sector of Berlin.

WHILE OTHER EAST PRUSSIANS tried to press on westwards, Peter Elxnat and the remainder of his trek made a huge detour southwards to Dresden in Saxony. His young wife, whose family came from Dresden, had given birth there to their first son a few days earlier.

Dresden had been devastated by bombs, however, and the trek could not stay there. Through his wife's family, Elxnat found an estate at Neukirchen, not far away, where he could leave his horses and wagons. His mares had all foaled along the way and the foals were alive and healthy, but tragically he had had to shoot them all to spare them a terrible death from cold, hunger or exhaustion. By chance he heard that some sires from Georgenburg had reached a nearby stud at Moritzburg and among them was Portwein, whom he had used to cover his mares before. He had Portwein brought to Neukirchen, his mares were covered and then worked in the fields. But then, after a few weeks, with the Russians approaching again, they had to flee once more.

IN OCTOBER 1944 Barbara von Sperber, with her six children and the remains of her trek, had arrived safely at her brother's estate in Nauendorf, Saxony. To her great astonishment and delight, the 80 horses she had left in Lenken had arrived ahead of her: someone, presumably a senior Wehrmacht officer, had read the note on her writing desk and done as she asked. Unfortunately the horses had travelled for several days and nights in open wagons with no fodder or water, and severe frost. They were very weak and several, particularly the yearlings, died of exhaustion or illness. Even then, the arrival of so many horses put an immense strain on the community. 'Bärbel, *nee, nee …*' fretted the local mayor, 'where am I going to put them all?' But with the help of friends, they were able to lend out the horses to farms and estates in the area to work in exchange for their keep.

The winter passed uneventfully. With the spring the Americans arrived to occupy their area but in May 1945 it was handed over to the Russians. Many of their horses were taken away or simply disappeared. They managed to hide their best mares in a barn, which was difficult because they had to remove many bales of straw in order to reach them and the horses gave their presence away by whinnying when other horses passed along a nearby road. They tried to hide them in the forest, but it was too muddy underfoot. They laid planks on the ground but these reverberated loudly when the horses moved around.

Soon it was their own lives that were at risk. As big

estate owners they were as much in danger as Jews had been under the Nazis. One day they received orders to pack their necessities; they were going to be taken away. Barbara played for time, at first refusing to go without her husband, who was away. They hid for a day or so, but realised that was futile. A friendly policeman who was supposed to be taking them off advised her quietly to leave some of her six children with friends. He protested in broad Saxon, 'Ee, ma'am, that's not right what they are doing to you.' The local parson's family took in her two youngest children, aged about four months and two years; the third was looked after by some kindly farmers in a nearby village. But the policeman became pressing; he would get into trouble if they delayed any further. They packed their belongings and themselves into a wagon and set off in a raging blizzard. The villagers were indignant, particularly at the sight of her old mother being taken away. 'That's no way to treat people ...' someone protested. The first stop was the Russian military commander's office, where they were told that this was a matter for the German authorities. They were sent to the German District Administrator, who thought it unfair that refugees should be treated this way and said if the mayor agreed, they could go home. He did agree, and, immensely relieved. they returned home, safe for the moment.

BUT THE EXPERIENCE had been a warning, and before long they were sitting in a lorry belonging to the local dealer in agricultural machines, heading for the border. From there they made their way across on foot.

LATE IN FEBRUARY Brigitte and her family had reached the estate of her husband's fellow officer at Bargensdorf, south of Neu-Brandenburg, where she had spent her honeymoon. His energetic wife, a convinced Nazi, insisted that they work for her – Amica was put to work in the fields and Brigitte had to give her children lessons. The food she provided was dismal, even by wartime standards.

Two months later the Russians had caught up with them and again they had to flee. They were about to set off, but their hostess was nowhere to be seen. They found her in her bedroom with her two children and a revolver in her hand. The energetic Nazi had cracked. She would never see her husband again, never see her home again; there was nothing left for them to live for, she sobbed. She wanted to put an end to it all.

There was not a moment to lose, but they could not let the children die. Slowly they managed to convince her that there was still hope and that she should give her children a chance. She eventually set off with them and they headed for her cousin's farm in Schleswig-Holstein.

Frau von Zitzewitz had halted her trek in western Mecklenburg and lent her horses to local farmers to work in exchange for their keep. Some had been stolen. By sheer chance, while buying oats in Hagenau one day in May 1945, she ran into an acquaintance, cavalry captain Botho von Berg. The British occupiers had put von Berg in temporary charge of Redefin stud farm not far away and he had a good relationship with the British officers. The occupation zones were about to be realigned and Mecklenburg was to be occupied by the Russians.

Frau von Zitzewitz was anxious to get her family and horses into the British or American zone. Von Berg spoke to the senior British officer, a Major Koenigstein, who in civilian life was a banker and a horseman himself. Major Koenigstein, who was possibly of German or Austrian descent, immediately laid on lorries to collect all her borrowed and stolen horses and brought them to Redefin, where numerous Trakehner stallions from Braunsberg had arrived. There, for three happy weeks they were in paradise – there was enough to eat for the families and the horses, the stables were clean and the horses were looked after as if they belonged there. They even had their names and pedigrees hanging over their stalls. But finally the day came for Mecklenburg to be handed over and, furnished with British passes, with Eberhard driving a wagon with the remains of their belongings and Erdmute on a three-year-old, leading several chestnuts, they set off for Schleswig-Holstein where the Major had found them temporary accommodation.

A few weeks earlier the two groups of Georgenburg and Braunsberg stallions that had set out across from Braunsberg across the Frische Haff, led by von Warburg and the army vet Ernst Arnold respectively, had reached Redefin. It had been a long, nightmarish winter journey across war-ravaged northern Germany. The horses had had neither enough to eat nor adequate shelter to rest, and yet, to Heling's astonishment, 161 out of the 240 arrived safely, among them 56 from Georgenburg. Some were put out to stud in Mecklenburg, a few were sold to the army and Heling, in his anxiety to get them to the west, had 20 dispatched on foot to Celle. Another group escaped to the west at the beginning of May – whether with or without the complicity of the British is not known – before the Russians could take over. Von Warburg was also able to take about 30 Braunsberg and Rastenburg stallions to stables near Celle.

Ernst Ehlert had been insisting for a long time that all the Trakehners should be sent to places beyond the river Elbe, since it was clear that this would soon form the border between the Russians and the western Allies. But Berlin would not allow it. He and his family had to go to Perlin in Mecklenburg and the remainder of the horses would be sent on to them.

Perlin, with its ivy-covered Schloss, had been a private estate until it was taken over by the army in 1936 and used as a depot for preparing and training future mounts. While Ehlert's and Heling's colleagues had made them and their horses welcome and as comfortable as possible in their *Landgestüte*, the resident army officers, despite promises, were less obliging. In any case, accommodation was scarce in the tiny village of 240 inhabitants and many families were living in extremely cramped and difficult conditions. Room was found for the family in the former estate manager's house, close to the Schloss. They were privileged compared with some of the Trakehnen staff, some of whom had no cooking facilities; however, even for them life was hard. There was a desperate shortage of fuel and the nearest towns where they could buy food were Wittenburg and Schwerin, 16 and 24 kilometres away respectively.

By the spring of 1945 around 350 horses from

Trakehnen itself had been assembled in Perlin. That was just under half the number that had left Trakehnen on foot in October. But the wartime conditions were taking a terrible toll. A number of brood mares that had been sent by rail from Silesia were suffering pitifully from undernourishment and exhaustion. Many of their foals had died from starvation in the womb. One mare was so weak she was unable to stand up and had to be shot at the station. The others, who had trotted the 65 kilometres from Trakehnen to Georgenburg without difficulty in October were scarcely able to make the 10 kilometres from the station to the military depot.

It was hard to keep the stud going. It had taken some time before Ehlert's office staff, especially chief cashier Waldemar Alshuth and his assistants, reached Perlin. They needed stable boys who were still with the Trakehnen treks, a blacksmith and other craftsmen. Eventually the staff trek from Preussisch Eylau arrived, and members were astonished to find that the stubborn *Obersattelmeister* Kiaulehn, the chief groom whom they had left behind with his box wagon in the snow, had arrived before them – without the wagon or any of his belongings.

In April 1945 the war reached Perlin. The Trakehnen staff could hear the thunder of battle both to the east and the west. Crowds of refugees streamed through the village, fleeing from the Russians towards the western Allies. In the early morning of 2 May, the sky was full of enemy planes and in the late afternoon American tanks rolled into view. Two American officers drove into the village in a jeep, arrested the senior military officers and took them away. The Trakehnen officials were left alone. Three days later American troops moved in and occupied Perlin. Ehlert, Lilli and the family were forced out of the estate manager's house to make room for them, and had to squeeze into even more cramped and uncomfortable accommodation.

On 8 May they heard the announcement that the war had ended. It was a relief, but made no difference to their lives at the time.

On 2 June the Americans moved out and the British took their place. They were more considerate, but the family still had to move frequently from one place to another and once they even found themselves living in a sheep shed, where they spread carpets over the bales of straw and made themselves comfortable with borrowed furniture on one side, while the sheep ruminated on the other. The only place they could cook was outside – fortunately it was the middle of summer.

Ehlert had hardly had time to adjust when disaster struck. The British had stored ammunition in a thatch-roofed barn near the Schloss and on the morning of 6 June, for unknown reasons, this exploded and burst into flames. The fire spread to an administrative building opposite and reduced eight barns and their contents to ashes. All the Trakehnen vehicles, many of which were packed full of fodder and equipment, were destroyed. It was a colossal blow – and not the last.

Towards the end of that month, a senior British officer told Ehlert that it was possible that Mecklenburg would shortly be handed over to the Russians, as had been secretly agreed between the Allies before the invasion of Germany began. Ehlert turned to the British commanding officer in the area, Brigadier Bolton, a horseman himself, who promised to do his best to get permission to send the Trakehners to the west. Meanwhile Ehlert and his staff debated whether to try and escape anyway. It would be a desperate move: there were no more trains, their wagons were destroyed and if they did set off on foot, they had no means of transporting the fodder the horses would need on the way. But Bolton returned and, in the name of his government, flatly forbade them to take the horses away. They were German state property and must remain as reparations for the Russians: the British authorities evidently did not see any reason to breach agreements with their Soviet allies.

At the same time, Bolton advised them that in any case it would be pointless even to try to get the horses out. The new border was already heavily guarded by British and Soviet troops, and they would be turned back. Nevertheless, he did his best and after much pleading and negotiating, he finally managed to extract one concession from his superiors. Not all Mecklenburg was to be turned over to the Russians. The Ratzeburg district, bordering on Schleswig-Holstein, was to remain British. Therefore a proportionate number of horses could also remain under British control. On 30 June, two Trakehner sires, Sporn and Häscher, and 27 brood mares – seven of them with new foals – accompanied by a number of Trakehnen staff, left with the British troops for the Ratzeburg area. With each horse went a note, written on the back of its pedigree, which could save its life. It stated that the horse existed 'for the purpose of preserving the blood of the Trakehner Stud' and must not be removed from its guardian.

The following day the Soviet occupiers moved into Perlin and all hell broke loose. Soldiers roamed the village day and night, raping and robbing the residents. People were evicted from homes and offices and forced to live in corridors and landings or stables and pigsties. Ehlert had to change lodgings several times, and each time they became more cramped and primitive. Trakehnen office documents and accounts that had been locked away in a remote stable were broken into and thrown around; many important papers were lost.

Alshuth, his wife, two daughters and five grandchildren had been living with other families in the village school, but at the end of August they were all thrown out to make way for the Soviet police. He, his wife and one daughter moved with two other families into the church. They all had to share one small stove, which was set up in the middle of the church. Many of the staff had not been paid because the bank accounts were frozen and the Trakehnen administration had no cash.

A minimum of law and order was eventually established among the troops after a senior Soviet officer moved into Perlin, but both the Trakehnen staff and the Perliners continued to be subjected to intense harassment. The military horse depot and the Trakehnen administration were merged and turned into a Soviet state farm, with Ehlert as its director and the head of the depot as his deputy. But within days they were both fired from their posts because of 'illness' – whether real or supposed is not known – and docked half their month's pay on trumped-up charges of having 'neglected' their duties. Since neither received any pay anyway, the fine was meaningless. They were replaced by a Soviet first lieutenant, and the staff and families were subjected to what amounted to forced labour. All the women had to work in the fields every day, including Sundays. They were promised wages in cash and kind, but they only once received any money, and then for only two weeks. The potatoes they were promised never materialised and the other food arrived in very small quantities – and they were obliged to pay for it, at exorbitant prices.

IT HAD BEEN CLEAR from the start that the Russians would take away the Trakehner horses. Soviet army veterinarians arrived and took charge of their care and feeding. Among other things they insisted that the horses should also be fed during the night. When Ehlert protested that that would be bad for their health, he was told that Germans did not know anything about horse breeding.

On 31 August 1945 the dreaded day came. The Trakehners and a number of the horses from the army depot were taken away, loaded onto trains and sent off eastwards. With them went irreplaceable, handwritten studbooks, almost 50 oil paintings of famous horses by well-known artists, the office machines and the stud's official rubber stamp. After more than 200 years of history, Alshuth reflected later, that was effectively the end of Trakehnen.

An overwhelming sadness befell the Trakehnen staff. Their beloved horses had been the centre of their lives and work, and now they were gone. For Ehlert it was a devastating loss from which, some suspect, he never fully recovered. Almost all his work of the past 14 years was undone.

Some of the staff found work elsewhere in the area, while others stayed in their crowded quarters and worked as labourers for the Russian state farm Perlin. But after several weeks it was announced that Perlin was to become a Soviet garrison. The entire population, apart from a few craftsmen that the Russians needed, was moved out and imposed on nearby villages, where the result was the same disastrous overcrowding as before.

Dr Ehlert instructed one of his staff, Otto Weber, to bury two metal boxes containing the remaining Trakehnen office documents in a secret place, which he did. Then on 19 November he put Lilli, her mother and brother into a Russian cart and drove them to the nearby town of Wittenberg, where there was a doctor. For in the overcrowded house where they had been living, a woman had died of typhus and it looked as if Lilli had caught it too. She had a raging temperature and her legs were so swollen that she could not wear shoes and could hardly walk. Although Lilli was still seriously ill, they decided not to go back to Perlin, but to flee to the west.

Lilli's mother had heard that goods trains that had brought coal to the British garrison in Berlin were returning westwards empty, but they did not know where to find them. For three days they drove in vain from one town to another, until finally, at night, they found one in the station in the town of Stendal. The British guard warned them emphatically that if they were discovered at the border they would be sent to Siberia. They decided to risk it and climbed in – her grandfather had to be pushed and pulled till they got him into their wagon – and slowly the train started moving.

It was cold and the moon shone brightly. Many other people jumped on to the train as it rolled very slowly westwards. At the border everyone kept totally silent. No one moved. Parents put their hands over the mouths of their children. They could hear the Russian soldiers walking past and banging the wagons with their rifle butts. The tension was almost unbearable. After what seemed an eternity, the train started moving again and soon they were in the little town of Vorsfelde, in the west.

There the Red Cross had set up a reception centre for refugees from the east. They were warmly welcomed and looked after, and given as much to eat and drink as they wished. They spent their first night in the station waiting room. They stayed for a while in a town near Hamburg with Werner Ehlert, Lilli's uncle, who was working as an interpreter and driver for the British. Here the sick Lilli was put to bed and slowly nursed back to health. But soon her grandfather decided to move to Hunnesrück, a cavalry establishment in Lower Saxony where the young stallions born in Trakehnen in 1943 had been evacuated. His place, he felt, was with the last of his horses.

Lilli's mother had hoped to start life afresh in Hamburg with her second husband. But she was refused permission to enter the city, so she and the children went to join Ehlert in Hunnesrück.

Back in Perlin, Waldemar Alshuth and his wife had found lodgings with kind, friendly people in a nearby village. But robbery and violence was mounting again, and on the night of 5 January 1946 six Soviet soldiers burst into their house, held them and their hosts at pistol and knife point and robbed them of all their jewellery, family papers, savings books, clothing and linen. The Alshuths decided to leave, and on 31 January joined a shipment of refugees heading for the west.

ALMOST A YEAR had passed since the Lehmanns had fallen into the hands of the Russians. The area of East Prussia where they were living had now become part of Poland, although the mill where Frau Lehmann and Elfriede worked was still run by Russians. Their father had been fighting on the Eastern Front, they had not heard from him for a year and assumed he was dead. And he, having seen what happened to the population in villages overrun by the Red Army, feared they were dead too.

But on 27 December 1945, by an almost miraculous roundabout route, Frau Lehmann and the children received a letter from him. He was living only about 60 kilometres away, but in the west. Thanks to a benign Russian boss at the mill, they were able to get permission to go and join him.

IN SPRING 1945, while Ehlert doubtless still believed his Trakehners were safe in Perlin and Heling was moving his stallions westwards, Gauleiter Erich Koch, whose actions were bringing death, destruction and untold misery to millions of people, had still been living in luxury and wielding his evil power in Königsberg. For although almost all East Prussia and lands to the west had been overrun, the East Prussian capital, a small area of land around it and the small port of Pillau were still in German hands, surrounded by the Russians. The Soviet Army had made an attempt at taking it earlier, but failed. For the moment there was an uncanny lull. The devastated city was teeming with refugees.

Not that Koch intended to run any risks. While rail connections were still open, he had sent two railway wagons full of valuables to the west. As much afraid of assassination by East Prussians as of death at the hands of the enemy, he moved around only in bullet-proof cars. In January he secretly left the city, where he could be bombed at any moment, and moved with his immediate staff into the best hotel in the port of Pillau. When that was hit by a bomb, he moved into a heavily fortified house in the village of Neutief, on the northernmost tip of the Frische Nehrung, across the waterway from Pillau. He kept a short-take-off Fieseler Storch aircraft at the ready and from the beginning of April had two icebreakers – the *Ostpreussen* and the *Pregel* – with their engines running at Pillau, ready for him to board and escape at a moment's notice. All the while he sought, through his messages and propaganda, to give the impression to Berlin and to the population that he was constantly engaged in the heroic defence of the city. Hitler summoned him to Berlin to report on the events in person. But Koch was not going to do anything of the sort. He had his wireless operators signal back that he was unable to travel: he had been injured during fighting.

By the third week in April the Soviets were closing in on Berlin. Koch realised that the game was almost up and concentrated now on saving his own skin. His staff radioed to the icebreakers to come and pick them up at Neutief, but the ships replied that Soviet submarines were in the channel and they could not cross. They were ordered to head for the fishing port of Hela on the tip of another spit of land further out to sea, opposite Gotenhafen, and pick Koch and his staff up there.

Koch, his staff and his heavily armed SS guard set off in cars along the narrow Nehrung road, ruthlessly ploughing their way through streams of refugees and soldiers. All at once they ran into chaos – some Soviet units were attempting to land from the sea and the refugees were fleeing in panic. The party abandoned their cars and fled on foot, trudging westwards into the night until soon after midnight they came to the little fishing village of Schievenhorst on the mouth of the Vistula. There lay an air traffic control vessel that for weeks had been ferrying refugees and wounded soldiers daily to Hela. Koch's SS men with machineguns went on board, hijacked the ship and the party set off for Hela, where the *Ostpreussen* and the *Pregel* were waiting for them.

A few days earlier in Pillau one of the wireless operators on the *Ostpreussen* had seen an SS officer come on board and give instructions that Koch's Mercedes, crates of wine, cigars and liqueurs be taken on board. Huge trunks, large quantities of food and the Gauleiter's two greyhounds followed. There was still plenty of room on board and hundreds of refugees, many sick and injured, waited desperately on the quay. But Koch's orders were explicit: no refugees on board.

In Hela, too, refugees and the wounded lay in the open on the quays waiting for ships to take them further westwards. But Koch, who had arrived on board with his aides, his SS guard and even more luggage, still would not allow anyone else on board. The head of a *Volkssturm* unit appealed to the Gauleiter to take them with him. 'Don't bother me with that shit!' Koch shouted.

Koch spotted a 10-year-old boy on board and demanded to know what he was doing there. Terrified, the boy revealed that his mother and brother were on board too. They were the family of the first engineer, who was trying to smuggle them out to safety. Koch ordered them to disembark immediately. 'Unless my family comes too this ship will not leave Hela,' the engineer replied coolly. The captain interceded with Koch and the family were allowed to stay – the only refugees on board.

All the while, to make Hitler believe Koch was still at his post, the ship's radio was sending 'top secret' messages and reports about the 'heroic resistance' around Königsberg, where last troops were fighting desperately to keep the Russians at bay in the hopes that the surviving civilian population could get away in boats. The transmissions continued until Koch heard on the radio that Berlin had almost been taken by the Russians and that Göring and Himmler had sought on their own initiative to negotiate surrender with the Allies, and been fired for their pains.

The *Ostpreussen* headed for Rügen, a large island off

the Baltic coast, but the island's commander refused them permission to land. It was the first sign that Koch's power was slipping away.

On 1 May 1945 the ship received the announcement of Hitler's death. The wireless operator brought it to the officers' mess where Koch and his staff were drinking heavily. The head of his staff read it out. No one stood up. Koch cleared his throat and said they would have to report to Grand Admiral Karl Dönitz, whom Hitler had nominated as his successor. The war in the west must be stopped and they must fight on in the east. The orderly brought more bottles.

During the night of 2 May the ship arrived in German-occupied Copenhagen. Koch, who had exchanged his brown Nazi uniform for civilian clothes, went ashore and was driven in the German police chief's car, guarded by machine-gun-toting Gestapo men, to the German headquarters. A few hours later he returned. He had been refused permission to stay in Denmark.

On the morning of 7 May, the *Ostpreussen* steamed into the Flensburg fjord. Mürwik, a naval suburb of Flensburg, was Dönitz's headquarters. Only a few hours earlier Dönitz had given orders for Germany's unconditional surrender. Koch demanded from Dönitz a submarine to take him forthwith to South America. Dönitz refused.

On board the *Ostpreussen* it was now every man for himself. The wireless operator later described the scene: 'Feverish activity broke out. Weapons, documents and brown uniforms were being hurled overboard, crates and suitcases dragged on to shore. The rats were leaving the ship. The adjutant had changed from an SS *Hauptsturmführer* to a friendly army captain who addressed us as "Du" and willingly signed discharge papers. He told us the Gauleiter would probably go to the government headquarters at Mürwik and continue to do his duty there.

'But in the midst of all this confusion Koch had disappeared.'

CHAPTER 11

The battle for survival: the post-war years

Slowly, wearily, skeletal from lack of fodder, they dragged their battered wagons and exhausted families into Schleswig-Holstein, Lower Saxony and Hesse. Seven hundred years after the first knights and settlers had set out for that distant land and mixed with Balts, Slavs and religious refugees to create a state and a history of their own, the Trakehners brought thousands of their descendants back to the heartland of Germany.

They had trekked for 1,000. even 1,500 kilometres, pulling loads of up to 2,000 kg through bitter cold, snow and ice, through the fires, the bombardments and the shooting. They had rarely had enough food or rest. Many had been pregnant and lost their foals. It had probably been the greatest test of endurance ever demanded of horses and the Trakehners had shown, as never before or since, what their breeding was worth.

Rarely can the bond between humans and horses have been so strong. The horses had saved the East Prussians from death, rape, imprisonment, deportation and forced labour. And the East Prussians had saved their horses. From then on their trek mares had a special place in the refugees' hearts and lives as they struggled to survive in their new surroundings.

But it was only a small minority of Trakehners that finally pulled in to the British and American zones of defeated Germany. Out of 56,000 registered Trakehners in East Prussia in 1944, less than 1,000 reached the west. The rest had been killed, stolen, seized as reparations, lost, left behind or simply stayed with their owners in Russian-occupied territory.

Of the core of the breed – the state-owned mares and stallions from Trakehnen and the East Prussian *Landgestüte* – even fewer reached the west. There were the 60 colts born in 1943 whom Ehlert had sent to Celle and the two stallions and 27 mares saved for him by Brigadier Bolton. Chief groom Otto Adomat from Zwion arrived in Celle riding the sire Julmond and leading 20 three-year-olds. Another 23 Georgenburg stallions including Pythagoras's son Totilas arrived on foot from Moritzburg, which, with the ones that had been sent by train, meant that 83 Georgenburg stallions had been saved. Hermann-Wilhelm von Warburg had arrived on horseback with eight stallions from Braunsberg. It was pitifully few, but with the privately owned Trakehners there were still enough to save the breed from extinction. In normal times, that is. But the times were anything but normal.

In a land already devastated by war, with millions of refugees and expellees flooding in from the east and food and housing desperately scarce, the East Prussians and their horses were extremely unwelcome. Local inhabitants, struggling with their own losses and suffering, did not want to know about, or simply did not believe, the far more terrible experiences of the East Prussians. Some told East Prussians that their problems were their own fault, that they should have stayed at home and made the best of life under the Russians. They often assumed that the haggard, unkempt, often ragged people arriving on the treks had always lived like that, that they were vagabonds and inferior beings, and they treated them accordingly. This treatment bred the beginnings of a deep bitterness among many East Prussians, which was to last at least a generation.

Even their horses, although long admired as the oldest and noblest breed in Germany, were unwelcome. Local state studs, breeders, riding schools and other equestrian organisations still preferred their own heavier local breeds, such as the Hanoverians and the Holsteiners, and for some time after the war there was a distinct resistance to the idea of buying, breeding or using Trakehners, or even helping them survive. As months passed Martin Heling formed the strong impression that the Trakehner community were being penalised, not just because they were refugees, but also because they were Prussians. 'Prussia was to be convicted, damned and made responsible for everything untoward which had happened, and to be excluded as far as possible from every discussion,' he recalled bitterly.

The first priority of the occupying powers was to keep the human population from starving, and horses were competing for land, oats and fodder with people and other livestock. Schleswig-Holstein and Lower Saxony in particular already had many studs and a large horse population. Orders went out to slaughter thousands of superfluous horses and, inevitably, the horses of the refugees who lacked land, money, roots and influence, were the most vulnerable. Horses were rounded up on farms and large numbers designated for slaughter. When the time came for Peter Elxnat's horses to be rounded up he harnessed all five of them to a wagon and disappeared off down the road. He did not return until the next day when the danger had passed. But many a small breeder's heart was broken as he watched the horses that had saved his life be taken off to the knacker's yard.

The struggle to save the horses began the moment the East Prussians arrived. Franz Scharffetter and his son Hans-Joachim had reached the horse-breeding town of Verden in Lower Saxony with 16 of their original 22 Trakehners and were forced to try and keep their horses alive by grazing them along the grass verges of roads and, when they could, stealing fodder for them from barns. But they soon had to sell some of them in order to keep the most valuable mares.

The huge Dohna–Sasse–Haedge-Medicus trek reached the district of Hoya, south of Bremen, where many of its members settled. With them came 31 brood mares from the Schlobitten and Prökelwitz studs, and 68 from the Logdau and Sabloczyn stables. Dohna arranged to lend his and the Sasses' horses to farmers whose own horses had been requisitioned by the army and were badly in need of replacements. The one condition was that the mares were only mated with purebred Trakehner sires. Their rent was 20 marks a month, to be paid in potatoes, apples, onions and other produce – so at least their owners had enough to eat. For Johanna Sasse the day their beloved horses were gathered together in a farmyard and the farmers came to pick which ones they wanted to hire, was the most terrible day since she had left home. As time passed, the Sasses' horses died or were sold off. Nothing remained of their stud.

About three weeks after they arrived and settled in, all the members of the Sasse–Haedge-Medicus trek attended Sunday service together at the village church in Thedinghausen, near Hoya, to give thanks for their deliverance.

DESPITE THE DESPERATE LACK of fodder, horses were valuable assets in those early years when there were still few cars, lorries or tractors, and petrol was extremely scarce. And once again the East Prussians and their horses became partners in survival, transporting people and goods from one place to another. Peter Elxnat started a small haulage business, his horses pulling huge loads of tiles, sand and other building materials for the construction sites that were springing up everywhere to provide housing for the refugees and homeless. Later he took over the management of two farms in the Oldenburg area.

Brigitte and her family had reached Schleswig-Holstein in May 1945, just after the war ended, and found refuge at Liensfeld, near Eutin. In September that year Brigitte gave birth in Eutin hospital to her daughter Sibylle.

Brigitte was to learn that her mother, who had left them after they were evacuated in the autumn of 1944 and gone to stay with a cousin in Cranz, had been thrown out by the Russians and ordered to return home. She set out on foot and is believed to have died of hunger and exhaustion on the way.

For the first year or more Brigitte's father, Emil Pflaumbaum earned enough for them to live on by providing a horse-drawn taxi service. With his mare Arkade harnessed to the dogcart, he drove Liensfeld people to Eutin and back.

Anna von Zitzewitz took over an abandoned farm, Hof Hambach, on the fringes of the former military training area of Bergen-Belsen in the Lüneburg Heath. There she was joined by the von Sperbers and their six children. But the conditions they lived in were appalling. The place had last been a horse clinic and since 1936 had been totally derelict. There were no windows or doors, and there were holes in the floor where the floorboards had been torn out to make posts to tie the horses to. There was no electricity, no water and the two women had to wash their children in the nearby stream. Exhausted by the trek and life in primitive and freezing conditions, Anna contracted severe pneumonia. But the farm had become a contact point for East Prussian refugees, and an East Prussian doctor cured her, while a carpenter who had wandered in searching for his family managed to rig up doors and windows to provide a minimum of shelter. With her characteristic energy and toughness, Anna soon set about rebuilding a home and a life for her children.

The local agricultural authorities had found her an estate where, she was told, 25 of her horses would be cared for. Trustingly, she left them there and, for lack of transport and telephone, was unaware that they were being totally neglected. Twenty-three of them died, either of starvation or disease, while others were said to have drowned when the Weser flooded the meadows. One of the two that survived was her mare Velegu, a granddaughter of Bulgarenzar, who went on to found one of the most important post-war Trakehner families.

THOSE FIRST POST-WAR years were extremely hard for all Germans, but particularly for refugees. There was little to eat and no heating, they were not allowed to leave their towns or villages without permission and in any case there was little transport, public or otherwise. East Prussians worked extremely hard to rebuild an existence but most hoped and expected that they would be able to return home before too long. It was often years before this hope died out and they realised they had lost their homes forever.

In those dark days a saviour appeared in the shape of a jovial, generous Swede called Dr Arvid Aaby-Ericsson. He had long been a Trakehner fan and after the end of the war got in touch with Dr Fritz Schilke, an East Prussian breeder, to see how he could help. He would send oats and blankets for the horses, badly-needed clothes and no less than 380 pairs of shoes for the penniless breeders and their families. He used his influence to have a number of Trakehner sires bought for the Swedish stud at Flyinge. Above all, with his infectious enthusiasm and optimism, he gave the breeders encouragement to carry on, despite all the difficulties.

In Hunnesrück the manager, who was a good friend of Ehlert's, gave the family a whole room – later two – to themselves. It was a luxury at the time, but nevertheless they still had to live like millions of other refugees in the early post-war years, with the rooms divided with blankets or curtains: sleeping, cooking and eating in one part, and receiving visitors in the other. And there were many visitors, particularly breeders and other acquaintances who had fetched up in the west and were seeking advice from the respected *Landstallmeister*.

Some of the Trakehnen staff had found their way to Hunnesrück too. Others went to various other *Landgestüte* and often found employment there. Dr Seyffert went to Traventhal, in Schleswig-Holstein. Martin Heling had followed his horses to Celle and immediately set to work with his characteristic energy.

The day he arrived in Celle, 8 April, Heling discovered an abandoned Wehrmacht commissariat near the stables, still full of food and top quality fodder for horses. Backed by *Landstallmeister* Korndorff he obtained permission from the local authorities to remove the fodder and all hands were put to work to transfer it to the stud farm before the British reached Celle, which they did on the night of 11 April. This solved their fodder problems for the time being, but on 19 April they were all put to work again, this time by the British to clean out and prepare the rooms and stables of the commissariat as a temporary camp for freed prisoners-of-war. The British seemed highly suspicious of the stud farm. Tanks took up position on the riding arena and a guard of one corporal and two or three men was mounted on the

Landstallmeister's house, and checked the number of stallions several times a day.

The French former prisoners soon left the commissariat and were replaced by 1,234 Jewish women who had been freed from the nearby Bergen-Belsen concentration camp. They were fed by the United Nations Relief and Rehabilitation Administration (UNRRA), but since most of the Celle staff were away with the sires on stud duty, the task of cleaning and other care fell mostly on the Georgenburgers and certain Celle inhabitants whom the British suspected of having been Nazis, and who were given particularly unpleasant and humiliating tasks. Just as local inhabitants could not grasp what the East Prussians had suffered, Heling did not seem to know or understand what kind of hell the women had been through, even though he could see the consequences. 'They were in an appalling and wretched state', he wrote later. They 'had become unaccustomed to any hygienic practices, they had apparently lost every sense of cleanliness, they cooked as best they could on the most primitive, home-made hearths and obeyed the calls of nature where they were lying, standing or walking. A revolting smell hung over the whole area.'

THE TRAKEHNER COMMUNITY, like all East Prussians, had fled westwards to save their lives, but also in the hopes of reasonably humane treatment. Those who reached the west, on the whole, received it. Local inhabitants, particularly in the Hanover area with its long-standing links with Britain, greeted the troops as liberators. But after five years of a war provoked by Germany, five years of their own wartime propaganda and, more recently, the horrifying discovery of the concentration and extermination camps, the British and American occupiers were not always willing or able to understand the complex reality of life under a totalitarian regime. While some were correct, humane and compassionate, others regarded all Germans as villains and were arrogant and bullying. Numerous Trakehner horses already owed their survival to British officers, and more would in the months to come. But there was a red-haired officer at Celle who would take sadistic pleasure in inventing impossible tasks for the Georgenburgers to perform, and an unpleasant and arrogant British veterinary officer who considered himself in charge of the Trakehners, treated the staff like scum and made trouble wherever he could.

Heling was compelled to hand over nine fine stallions to British generals and officers as riding horses for their leisure hours, and all 23 thoroughbred racing horses from the Hoppegarten racing stables, which had fled from the stud farm at Graditz, were appropriated en bloc by the British military so they could hold their own races. (They were returned some years later.) Officers helped themselves to saddles, harness, stable equipment and fodder. One blatantly stole Heling's own saddle before his eyes. A hunting rifle that his father had given him when he had passed his school-leaving exams and which had been confiscated along with military weapons, was never returned. An extremely stuck-up Major from one of the Royal Horse Guards regiments took away 10 black stallions, which were later spotted taking part in the Trooping of the Colour in London.

This acquisitiveness may be partly explained by the fact that the British were entirely unfamiliar with the concept of state-run breeding and, since the stud staff wore uniforms, may have assumed they were a military establishment. But, Heling remarked later, such incidents 'did not strengthen one's willingness to come to terms with the fact that we had been totally defeated in a war that we had provoked'.

At the same time one British major, who was extremely knowledgeable about horses and appeared to be a breeder himself, was full of admiration for a group of three-year-old Trakehner stallions he saw at Celle, and for their training and the way the stable boys handled them. This clearly did not fit in with his picture of the Germans. 'People who are so kind to horses can't be Nazis!' he remarked.

The greatest friend of the Trakehners among the British, however, was a Major Whitecombe, the official of the British Military Government responsible for horse-breeding matters. Only four days after the war ended, the Major appeared at the Celle stud and introduced himself. Over a cup of tea in *Landstallmeister* Korndorff's apartment he explained that outwardly he had to abide by the occupiers' rule of 'no fraternisation'. But in reality, he said, all true horsemen were friends. And indeed he proved a good friend to the Trakehner community. Soon afterwards the process of denazification began and while Heling had a clean slate, von Warburg, Korndorff and some other *Landstallmeister* were sacked and in some cases imprisoned because they had belonged to SA or SS organisations, mainly the equestrian associations which

Gustav Rau had fought to prevent being taken over by the Nazis. Whitecombe intervened and had them released. Heling was made *Landstallmeister* of Celle, although in practice, by mutual agreement, Korndorff remained in charge. Later Heling was made *Landstallmeister* in Harzburg.

WITH ONE OF THE TREKS that pulled into Schleswig-Holstein in May 1945, with his wife, six-year-old son and other relatives, was the East Prussian breeder Dr Fritz Schilke. Schilke was the secretary-general of the East Prussian Studbook Society and as such had arranged for a couple of thousand horses to be sent to Mecklenburg and Pomerania – not far enough west, as it now turned out. As he reached Schleswig-Holstein, his trained eye immediately spotted a number of good Trakehner mares in the area. With immense determination, given the desperate conditions in those months, he decided that the homeless and poverty-stricken Trakehner breeders must be helped and their horses saved from slaughter. The breed must not be allowed to die out.

He borrowed two sturdy Trakehner chestnuts from a refugee farmer's wife, harness from relatives and a carriage from the stud at Traventhal. With this he toured the area, tracking down breeders. Soon he had built up a small network, which grew to around 600 – still much less than half its former size – and started a register of surviving Trakehners. Luckily, he too found horse-lovers among the British military government and was given permission and encouragement to try and save the Trakehner breed. His headquarters was in

Wiemerskamp, a village north of Hamburg, in the single room in which he and his family lived, slept and ate. The President of the Society, Baron Siegfried von Schrötter, also arrived in Wiemerskamp and for a time lived and worked in a horsebox parked nearby. There they also looked after the Trakehner mares that Brigadier Bolton had helped to save.

But at first theirs looked a hopeless task. The Society had no money – nearly one million marks it had held in bank accounts in the east was now effectively inaccessible. Few foals had survived the trek and, apart from Peter Elxnat's Polarstern, conceived on the way, there were none in 1946, nor in 1947. East Prussians hoped and believed that somehow they would soon be able to return home as they had after the First World War, and breeders were unwilling to burden their mares with another pregnancy for the return journey. Only in 1948 when it sank in that their return was not imminent, were Trakehner foals were born again.

Besides, the infrastructure needed to maintain and perpetuate a breed in Germany was lacking, such as organisations for marketing horses, licensing sires and training both breeders and horses. Scattered all over the country from the North Sea to the Alps, they lacked the protection of and long-standing connections to, a local government, agricultural boards and assorted equestrian organisations that local breeders enjoyed. As the new West German Federation took shape, the Trakehners fell between two stools – horse-breeding, like most of agriculture, fell under the jurisdiction of the Land, or state, governments but these would argue that the Trakehners, being spread all over the country, were a matter for the federal government.

It was soon obvious that if the breed were to be saved, new solutions would have to be found. There was no way of recreating the structures – the *Hauptgestüt* at Trakehnen and the various *Landgestüte* – that had been the pillars of the Trakehner breed. At the same time however, without larger centres where breeding could be carried out systematically, the Trakehner would have no future.

On 27 October 1947 the East Prussian Studbook Society held its first and last meeting after the war. The 120 members who came voted to cease its activities and immediately to found the Association of Breeders and Friends of the Warmblood Horse of Trakehner Descent as its legal successor. It was known from then on by its shorter name, the Trakehner Association.

Thanks to efforts by Martin Heling and Alexander von Dohna, a small stud was founded at Erichsburg, a farm attached to Hunnesrück, with space for 50 mares and four sires under the care of Dr Ehlert. It was financed partly by the federal government, partly by that of Lower Saxony. Many of the 28 mares saved from Perlin were established there and private breeders were allowed to send up to five mares to be kept there – although most could send only one. As payment every second foal from each mare was to remain the property of the Trakehner Association, which slowly built up a valuable herd. Nevertheless fodder was badly lacking at first and some of the mares, already weakened by the journey, died.

Deals were made with two Schleswig-Holstein

landowners, Prince Moritz of Hessen and Count von Baudissin, to create two more studs on their private estates. Twenty-five mares and a couple of sires were housed at Schmoel, Prince Moritz's estate by the Baltic sea, and the mares earned their living by working on the land. The foals were raised until they were three years old and again every second foal of each mare went to the estate. By the time the contracts expired after 10 years, the estates had excellent Trakehner herds of their own for little financial outlay. The Trakehner Association later leased the whole operation at Rantzau and used it as a specialised stud to raise young stallions.

Sadly, the great sire Pythagoras had disappeared during the war, and it was never known what became of him. But his son Totilas became one of the most important sires in the rebuilding of the breed at Rantzau. There too for a time were Brigitte's mare Amica and her father's Arkade. In Schmoel were Kassette and Cancara's daughters, Donna and Kokette, from the mixed herd at Trakehnen. The sires Sporn and Häscher, saved from Perlin, and Julmond, who brought Otto Adomat to safety in the west, fathered numerous excellent foals.

Photographs of the irresistibly appealing face and huge, melting eyes of a young Trakehner foal with the caption '*Wer nimmt mich?*' ('Who will take me?') appeared in newspapers and magazines, an imaginative campaign by the Association to seek foster parents to raise Trakehner foals. Under this initiative, private horse lovers with the necessary land and infrastructure would receive two foals free of charge. One would be handed back to the owner after a couple of years, while the other would remain the foster parent's property. The campaign was a great success and there were always more would-be foster parents than there were available foals.

IF THE START had been hard in the west, it was even worse behind the Iron Curtain, where many Trakehners and the people associated with them remained. East Prussians and their horses were no more welcome in the Soviet-controlled zone of Germany than in the west. They too suffered from hunger and homelessness, but also from the various whims of the political regime. For the Communist leadership horses had been the preserve of the rich and land-owning classes rather than the peasants or workers, and therefore associated with what they called 'warmongers' and 'class enemies'. Trakehners, particularly, were associated with Junkers and were therefore doubly suspect. Horses were often victims of the immense upheavals that were being imposed on society in general and farmers in particular.

One East Prussian farmer and his wife had trekked as far as the Mark Brandenburg with two of their Trakehners. With their son, who had just returned from the war, they were given seven hectares to cultivate, a cow and a heifer. The land could not support two horses so, heartbroken, they had to give one away. They had built their own house and were proud that they had made their land productive and were fulfilling their production targets. Soon, however, they and other farmers in the area were forced under massive pressure to 'voluntarily' join the local collective farm. The land was no longer theirs. The authorities took away two of their – by then – three cows. The horse was not wanted; it was strong and hardworking, but was 18 years old and the collective farm did not take older horses.

The horse and its companion had brought them out of East Prussia. It had saved their lives, but they could no longer feed it. They begged for fodder from other farmers, but they had none either and were having to take their own horses to the slaughterhouse. The horse got thinner and thinner, and the farmer himself became thin and ill. Not being able to stand the sight of his starving animal, he dreaded going into the stable. The son tried to find someone to give the horse to, but no one could take it. There was no alternative: early one morning people came to take it to the slaughterhouse. The wife stood weeping at the window; the son went into the fields so he could not see it go. When he returned that evening, there was no sign of his father. They found him in the stable where the horse had stood; he had hanged himself.

THE TRAKEHNER BREED, like Germany itself, became divided. It was still possible to breed Trakehners in Communist East Germany – just. However, it took immense strength of character, determination and personal courage to cope with the immense political and bureaucratic obstacles. And luck, too, for the ideological wind could suddenly change and there were pitfalls everywhere. The head of the Neustadt livestock breeding office, Gustav Condereit, persuaded the Soviet authorities to let him restart the stud. He scoured the countryside for breeding horses, as well as ordinary horses that he could later exchange for better ones. He found the Trakehnen sire Hexenschuss, a son of Dampfross, in a pitiful condition on a farm. The farmer had bought him from Russian soldiers for two bottles of vodka. Condereit bought him, nursed him back to health and Hexenschuss went on to father valuable Trakehner foals.

Condereit paid a substantial sum of money for Hexenschuss, but often he was able to persuade farmers to relinquish horses in exchange for cows or sheep, a form of barter that was Condereit's downfall. He was arrested by the East German police and charged with economic crimes. His daughter Hannamarie persuaded the Soviet military authorities in Berlin to intervene and he was released. However, a few years later he was in trouble again for opposing the regime's plans to collectivise agriculture, and in 1953 he fled to the West.

Soon farms everywhere were being forcibly collectivised and mechanised and many thousands of other farmers were being obliged to part with their horses. The horse population was decimated and breeding thrown into a severe crisis.

Only in around 1970 would the regime wake up to the fact that horse-riding was booming in the West and that much-needed hard currency could be earned by breeding and selling cheap horses. The *Landgestüte*, particularly Neustadt, underwent a revival. Many of these horses, 80 per cent of which went to West Germany alone, were of indifferent quality, but at least horse breeding was acceptable again. In 1969 the authorities were persuaded to conduct a census of Trakehner horses – those with papers or ones bearing either the single or double elk's antler brand. Over a hundred of them were gathered together at a new state farm at Ganschow in Mecklenburg; the number later rose to nearly 700. Bureaucratic interference often meant that poor-quality mares were included, but they also had the valuable cooperation of the Kirov stud, with its original Trakehner herd. Despite all the difficulties, Ganschow produced some excellent Trakehners.

FOR THE TRAKEHNER COMMUNITY the fact that relatively few of their horses reached the west was a great blow. But as horse people they would be relieved to learn later that many of those from Trakehnen itself and the *Landgestüte* that had been seized by the Red Army, had actually survived. Between April and October 1945, a total of 1,145 Trakehners were shipped to the Soviet state stud farm in Kirov on the river Don – 435 stallions, 350 mares, 201 yearlings and 157 unweaned foals, among which, remarkably, were 15 surviving orphans. Many of them were from the original Trakehnen herds.

Most of the stallions were then sold off in different parts of the Soviet Union and it is not known what became of them. The rest continued to be bred in Kirov, which was for many years the only Trakehner stud in the Soviet Union. (The 5,000 that had been sold off by the East Prussians to the Soviet Union after the First World War appear to have been killed or dispersed during the fighting in the Second.)

TODAY, 65 YEARS after the East Prussian apocalypse, Trakehners are once again a world-renowned breed.

They owe it largely to the passion and tenacity of their East Prussian owners and guardians, who battled against immense odds to prevent them from dying out in the west. They are now an international breed, with studs in more than 30 countries, from Canada and the United States to Siberia and Brazil. They remain among the most coveted riding and competition horses and regularly win top medals in the Olympics and leading international equestrian events.

In Germany the Trakehner is still the smallest of the main breeds, due to its lack of a regional base, but there are nonetheless 2,800 breeders with 4,500 registered brood mares and 280 sires, which together produce around 1,600 registered foals a year.

At the same time, Trakehners have greatly influenced other breeds. Trakehner stallions have been used to improve and refine other breeds as the demand for riding horses soared and the need for heavier draught horses almost vanished. But the Trakehner itself remains a 'closed' breed, its registered mares to be mated only with its registered sires. The only new blood allowed in from outside is, as ever, English thoroughbred and Arab.

Horse-lovers can debate for hours the qualities of present-day Trakehners. Some, particularly old East Prussian breeders and those from former Communist-ruled territories, believe that nowadays money has too much influence in selection and breeding. If so, this is surely not limited to the one breed. But the calculated rigour in selecting sires and mares and the strenuous testing with obstacle courses, hunts and steeplechases, which produced such superb horses in Trakehnen, is hard to reproduce today. At the same time, Western breeders may sometimes look down, often unfairly, upon the results of problem-fraught breeding in the east.

The descendants of the core herd from Trakehnen are flourishing in Russia. Until the 1960s they were limited to the state stud in Kirov, where they were in the hands of excellent horse people and breeders. Now there are private Trakehner studs in many regions. At the beginning the breed is said to have suffered from being crossed with others as a result of the now-discredited theories of the late Soviet geneticist and Stalin protégé, Trofim Denisovic Lysenko. But today Russian Trakehners are widely admired, including by the leading Trakehner experts in Germany. They are rangier and lighter than German Trakehners and, because of the climate, are even hardier than those in the West. Russian Trakehners have covered themselves in glory in international events. Particularly memorable are two sons of Pythagoras, Pepel and Ikhor, both of which won Olympic Gold and Silver medals.

One sometimes hears, in both Germany and Russia, that the Trakehners in East Prussia were requisitioned and taken to Russia on the orders, or at least at the instigation of, Marshal Semyon Mikhailovitch Budenny. Budenny had been a First World War cavalry hero, Inspector (chief) of the cavalry and was in charge of Soviet horse breeding before becoming a less-than-successful commander in the Second World War. He founded the eponymous breed of Budenny horses and was certainly very interested in the Trakehner. The author has, however, been unable to find any trace of such an order.

In 1994, 50 years after the end of Trakehnen, a delegation from the German Trakehner Association paid a visit to Kirov. They branded foals of pure Trakehner pedigree with the double elk's antler and burnt the same mark into the wood of the stables, the sign that Trakehners are bred there. It was not so much reconciliation for – as Lars Gehrmann, the general manager points out – being horse-lovers, they could not be angry with the Russians who had preserved many of the original Trakehner herd. Instead it was the beginning of a friendship that had been hindered for half a century by the Iron Curtain.

The Poles, great horse-breeders, had been using Trakehners since long before the war. Afterwards they bought all but 11 of the stallion colts that Ehlert had succeeded in shipping to Celle, received others as part of war reparations and collected together more that they found wandering around ownerless after the war ended. These were bred, at first under extremely difficult conditions, primarily in the former East Prussian stud at Liesken (now Liski) under the name of the Polish Masurian Horse (Kon Mazurski). Another respected Polish breed, the Wielkopolski, has much Trakehner blood.

EAST PRUSSIA, as such, no longer exists. After the war relatively few Germans remained to see people being brought in from the Soviet Union and Poland to repopulate the region and they too were forced to leave a couple of years later. Soon a near-straight border ran through the middle of it between the Rominten Heath (Puszcza Romincka) in the east and the Frische Haff near

Heiligenbeil (Mamonovo). To the north is the Kaliningrad Oblast, which is an enclave of Russia. The southern half is now part of Poland. The towns and villages – or what remained of them – were given Russian or Polish names. Königsberg became Kaliningrad, Insterburg became Cernyahovsk, and Gumbinnen became Gusyev. Until the fall of Communism, the Russian part was a closed military area and out of bounds to foreigners.

Trakehnen is now called Jasnaya Polyana – 'bright glade' – but it is a desolate place. Where Lilli once walked along carefully swept paths with neat fences, surrounded by trees and hedges and smooth green sward, is now a wasteland of weeds and rubble. Rusting corrugated iron, hideous chimneys and the ugly wreckage of a Communist-era collective farm litter former paddocks and parks. The land is only partly cultivated, the canals that Friedrich Wilhelm's soldiers dug to drain the land are neglected and overgrown. Much is returning to nature and with time could become the marshland that it was before Trakehnen's story began.

By no means the entire complex was destroyed in the war, but it almost might have been. The long red-brick stables where Helmut Hufenbach and Otto Fiege once groomed their horses under the eagle eye of *Obersattelmeister* Kiaulehn now stand empty and derelict, the roofs collapsed in places from neglect, tiles littering the ground. 'It did not need a war to do this,' remarked a Russian visitor. 'Just bad politics, bad economics.'

The great oak that stood in front of the *Landstallmeister*'s Schloss is still there, older and thinner and gnarled. On the plinth where the bronze statue of

Tempelhüter once stood, is the carved head of a soldier wearing a helmet – a war memorial. The white arch over the lane to the Schloss still stands and local people, brought in from various parts of the Soviet Union after the war to repopulate the area, believe that if you stand underneath it and make a wish, it will come true.

One imagines that many may make a wish to leave. For although the local community seems to be warm and close-knit, there is little work and little hope for many of them at present in Trakehnen. Children who do well at school, one is told, tend to go away and never come back. The former collective farm is now a limited company and its crops have improved. But much produce is imported and throughout the rest of former East Prussia, much of which is also now uncultivated, it is scarcely worthwhile to try and work the land. Bad politics, bad economics …

The Schloss still stands, for it has long been used as the village school. A 160-member German association set up to help Trakehnen has restored the crumbling building and renovated its façade. It has installed new windows there and in the stable boys' house, now also part of the school, and is trying to raise money to repair the roof and provide better sanitary facilities. Dr Ehlert's old office on the ground floor is now a little museum where visitors can learn about the history of the place.

The association has invited groups of children from Trakehnen to Germany three times, for exchanges with a school in Walsrode on the Lüneburg Heath and for trips round the country. Children from Walsrode have been to Trakehnen. The initiative was a great hit on both sides and seems set to become a regular feature of each school's calendar.

The statue of the great sire Tempelhüter now stands outside the Russian horse museum in Moscow. In 1974 an original bronze copy cast from it was placed outside the German horse museum in Verden.

The huge stud farms at Weedern and Georgenburg have risen again. At Weedern a Russian company led by Jelena Baturina, the wife of the Mayor of Moscow, has lavishly restored or rebuilt the stables and other buildings and is restoring the Schloss, which is to be turned into a luxury hotel. Erdmute von Zitzewitz has provided old photographs, plans and recollections to help with the work. She is frequently invited there and relations are very friendly. A Russian company led by an oil magnate has similarly transformed Georgenburg, and given it back its German name. Now international show jumping events are held there in September.

The Frische Haff is a haunting stretch of water, the preserve of fishermen who would like to make more money by giving boat rides to tourists. Its bed is a hunting ground for divers who sell what they find: old military equipment and the contents and wreckage of wagons. A good skull can fetch 20 dollars on the black market.

Since the Russian part became accessible, some East Prussians have been back, often to find little or nothing of their former homes standing.

Peter Elxnat's father's guns remain in their hiding place.

Epilogue

On 25 May 1949, a man with a beard and dark glasses who claimed to be Rolf Berger, a retired Luftwaffe major and former estate owner in Gumbinnen, was arrested near Hasenmoor, north of Hamburg, and handed over to the British. In his pocket was a cyanide capsule similar to those that had been issued to top Nazis towards the end of the war. Göring and Himmler, among others, had made use of them to avoid being hanged by the Allies.

Erich Koch, former master of fabulous palaces, multimillionaire and governor of lands from the Baltic to the Black Sea, had been in hiding on a farm near Hasenmoor. He appeared to have scratched a living as a labourer and occasionally as a sales representative, but had also been on the dole. He had separated from his wife Kläre, who had moved in with his former adjutant. Curiously, Koch had gone to ground in one of the areas where there were most East Prussians and therefore where he was most likely to be recognised. But he seems to have felt safe – possibly because he had already passed in and out of a British prisoner-of-war camp with forged papers without being recognised. Perhaps he was protected by diehard Nazis or perhaps, even after his fall, he had remained out of touch with reality. For whatever reason, he seems to have even felt secure enough to attend an East Prussian reunion; there an East Prussian tipped him off that he had been recognised and urged him to flee. But Koch did not want to. His reason: he had just bought a pair of rabbits and now had a chest of drawers to put his clothes in.

A British court extradited him to Poland, where he was wanted for the mass murder of Jews and members of the Polish intelligentsia in extermination camps and for the burning of villages, some as reprisals for the killing of Germans and others to make way for hunting ranges for Göring. He was accused of setting up concentration camps and summary police courts, of plunder, mass deportations of Poles to slave labour, and other crimes. The accusations against him filled 12 court volumes – and these only concerned the districts of Bialystok and Ciechanow, which had been annexed to his *Gau* (region) of East Prussia. The Soviet authorities withdrew their extradition request for much vaster crimes in Ukraine in favour of the Poles.

Koch was held in Warsaw's Mokotow prison, where the SS had tortured and murdered innumerable Poles and was later, ironically, to complain to the court that it was 'hell'. By dint of hunger strikes, an alleged suicide attempt and various – possibly self-inflicted – illnesses, Koch succeeded in dragging out the start of the trial for eight years. When he was finally judged fit enough to stand trial he appeared in court a ghastly wreck of his former self. Apparently scarcely able to walk, he shuffled into the courtroom in felt slippers, supported by two policemen. He was emaciated, his cheeks sunken, his hair long and unkempt, his former toothbrush moustache now long and droopy. He would slouch half-lying in the dock with his eyes closed, taking pills passed to him by a nurse and belching loudly every few minutes. Sometimes he would attend lying on a stretcher, at other times in an armchair with his feet up on a stool and a blanket around his legs, a mug of tea to hand. His condition appeared at least partly to be feigned because his remarks, in a firm voice and fully-formed sentences, showed that he was in full possession of his faculties and was following the trial closely.

Koch maintained his complete innocence. The SS and police were not under his command and he had no responsibility for their actions, he claimed. It was all the fault of others. He claimed to be 'shattered' by what Germans had done in Poland but denied being one of the culprits. He had fought the SS and saved the Poles from much worse. It was thanks to him that so many East Prussians had been able to flee over the Haff. He expected, he stated, to be acquitted.

On 9 March 1958, after what was agreed in the West to have been a fair trial in Warsaw, Erich Koch was found guilty of murder and complicity in murder of 400,000 people and of crimes against humanity. He was sentenced to death. As the sentence was read Koch collapsed on to his court bench and covered his face in a handkerchief. He was never held to account for his many appalling crimes in East Prussia or Ukraine.

As he appeared to be gravely ill at the time, the Polish court suspended the execution. Koch lived on, in his latter years a privileged prisoner who assiduously read the Bible, much German literature and publications sent from the West. These, and food he had sent from the

West, were reportedly paid for out of DM14.6 million he had raised from the sale of land in West Germany. According to the Polish prison authorities, he refused to clean his own cell. He kept himself fit, taking plenty of exercise and medicines prescribed by the prison doctor. He remained a convinced Nazi and insisted to the end that there was no blood on his hands.

He died on 12 November 1986, aged 90.

ERNST EHLERT stayed in Hunnesrück looking after his beloved horses. He was regarded by everyone in the horse world as the grand old man of breeding, although he withdrew into the background. The leadership of the Trakehner community passed to Schilke, Heling and others. Ehlert longed to return to East Prussia, but did not live to see it again. He died in 1957 aged 82.

Lilli's mother lived with him in Hunnesrück until he died. Lilli herself moved to Hanover in 1952, trained to be a children's nurse and worked in a paediatrician's surgery until she married in 1957.

Martin Heling became the head of the Department for Studs and Horse Breeding under the British Military Government and subsequently held the equivalent post in the government of Lower Saxony. He periodically suffered from severe stomach and other ailments as a result of the privations during and after his flight to the west. In 1950 he became *Oberlandstallmeister* of Lower Saxony. Four years later he retired and died in 1982.

Hermann-Wilhelm von Warburg, former *Landstallmeister* of Braunsberg, became general manager of the Central Association for Breeding and Testing Warmblood Horses and secretary-general of the Hanover Racing Association. He died in 1971, aged 70.

Gustav Rau, the famous horse expert who fell foul of the Nazis, became *Landstallmeister* at Dillenburg and continued to exercise much influence in the horse world in the post-war years.

Hans Seyffert also fled to the west and fetched up at the *Landgestüt* Traventhal, near Bad Segeberg in Schleswig-Holstein. But although he was only around 50 at the time, he withdrew from the world of breeding and went into retirement, a disappointed man. It is possible that his membership of the SS prevented him from holding any further posts. He was also accused after the war of not having done enough to save the Trakehners, a charge refuted both by former colleagues and by the records. He lived quietly with his family in Bad Segeberg, suffering from an eye complaint and, according to one account, periodic bouts of depression. He died in 1968.

Hans Güntzel, the *Landstallmeister* of Neustadt, was released from the Soviet transit camp after a couple of months and was given shelter with his crippled wife by the Neustadt parish. Just as he had been unable to grasp that Germany was losing the war, he was now unable to cope with what had befallen him. Shattered by his experiences in the camp and by the loss of his social status, his work and his possessions, he wasted away and died in abject poverty two years later.

Obersattelmeister Kiaulehn reached the west and settled near the former *Landgestüt* at Traventhal, where he died.

Helmut Hufenbach remained in Perlin for a time,

working for the Russians, then moved to Saxony to live near relatives. He later settled in Schönfeld, Pomerania, and worked on a farm.

Barbara von Sperber moved to Eltville in the Rheingau, where her husband worked in the cement industry. In 2003 she celebrated her 90th birthday with her seven children, their spouses and some of her numerous grandchildren. She died in 2006.

Anna and Erdmute von Zitzewitz were obliged to leave Hof Hambruch in 1962, when the area again became a military training ground. They settled at Katherinental in Schleswig-Holstein, where they continued to breed Weedern Trakehners. Anna died in 1968 and Erdmute carried on her parents' work. In 2002 she handed over most of her horses to a relative to continue the breed and that year spent her 70th birthday in Weedern, participating in a television documentary about East Prussia.

Peter Elxnat settled in Hohenkirchen, near the North Sea coast, and became another important contributor to the revival of the breed. His trek mare Filiale, whom he had had covered by Portwein at Moritzburg during the trek, gave birth to the first Trakehner foal to be born after the war in West Germany. It was named Polarstern, who then became the first Trakehner stallion to be licensed after the war. Polarstern was sent as a reserve to the 1952 Olympics in Helsinki, but was not allowed to participate because he was too young. He later became a main sire at the famous Swedish stud farm at Flyinge. Filiale's half-sister Schwindlerin founded one of the most important post-war Trakehner dynasties, producing no less than 10 daughters and 42 granddaughters who became brood mares and who between them produced around 20 selected stallions.

Peter Elxnat died in 2007. His work is being continued by his son Walther, who is now the sixth generation of Elxnat Trakehner breeders. His grandchildren are also showing an interest in breeding.

Johanna Sasse, now Johanna Deicher, had herself apprenticed to a seamstress in their village, then learned haute couture in Frankfurt and became a highly qualified dressmaker. She opened an atelier in Hanover and built up a flourishing business making clothes for high society.

Otto Fiege became a professional show jumper, first for the East German border guards' equestrian team and later for the secret police team, and was the East German show jumping champion in 1959 and 1960. When the East German state and military organisations closed down their show jumping activities, he became a trainer.

After the war Brigitte Boettcher moved with her husband to Ziegelhausen, near Heidelberg, where he and his sister built up a jewellery firm. Her father, Emil Pflaumbaum, leased some land and stables at Liensfeld and continued a small but very successful breeding activity with their mares Amica, Arkade and Salamanca. Amica lived to be 24 and produced many excellent foals.

Gerd Lehmann studied agriculture and became *Landstallmeister* in Warendorf. He retired in 1995.

Franz and Hans-Joachim Scharffetter leased a farm in the Bremen area in 1950 and once again became successful breeders. Franz died in 1978 at the age of 81.

Hans-Joachim now has his own farm in Schwanewede-Brundorf, where he breeds horses and keeps cattle.

After the fall of Communism, the remaining Trakehnen office documents that had been buried by Otto Weber somewhere in the Soviet-occupied zone were dug up by his younger brother, Ewald. Despite some water damage, many of them were still intact. They were bought by a Bavarian Trakehner breeder, Hans-Ernst Wezel.

The last surviving horse born in Trakehnen, the chestnut sire Keith, who had stood in Harzburg and Celle, died in private ownership in 1977 aged 36.

Acknowledgements

It has been said that the true witnesses to this terrible chapter in modern history are the dead. But it is the survivors who have passed on to us a picture of the almost unimaginable suffering, the fear, the courage and the endurance of many in those weeks and months of the great flight. I am most grateful to all those East Prussians who have shared their often painful memories with me: Brigitte Boettcher, Johanna Deicher, Hans Klein, Peter Elxnat, Helmut Hufenbach, Otto Fiege, Gerd Lehmann, Hans-Joachim Scharffetter, Uli Scharfenorth, Barbara von Sperber and Erdmute von Zitzewitz. My deep regrets to those whose stories, for reasons of space, I was unable to use, and to other survivors whom I was unable to contact.

I am also deeply indebted to Lars Gehrmann of the Trakehner Verband (Trakehner Association); Britta Stühren of the Deutsches Pferdemuseum (German Horse Museum) in Verden; Christoph Hinkelmann of the Ostpreussisches Museum (East Prussian Museum) in Lüneburg; Karola Wagner of the Bundesarchiv (Federal Archives); and Renate Maczka of the Nord-Ost Bibliothek (Library of the North-East), Lüneburg; to Mischa Bykoff, Alexandra Gräfin Dohna, Anna Vitalievna Dorofeeva, Klaus Hagen, Joachim Gusovius, Miriam Lenz, Ulrike Lutz, Patricia Meehan, Jürgen Müller, Elena Plath,

Angelika Volle and Hans-Ernst Wezel. Special thanks to Erhard Schulte, Gerd Lehmann and Martin Mantzke for kindly combing the manuscript for historical errors.

Glossary

Bauernnotbewegung – Farmers' Emergency Movement, a sometimes violent protest movement

Gauleiter – all-powerful Nazi party official in charge of a region

Greifkommando – Nazi press gang

Hauptgestüt – main state stud farm, where a breed was developed and perfected

Junker – owners, often aristocratic, of large estates in eastern Germany

Landgestüt – Regional state stud farm, whose purpose was to serve farmers' and private owners' mares

Landstallmeister – Director of a main state stud farm (e.g. Trakehnen) or of a regional state stud farm (e.g. Georgenburg or Braunsberg)

Luftwaffe – German air force

Oberlandstallmeister – Master of Horse, or government official responsible for all state horse breeding in Germany

Obersattelmeister – Chief groom in charge of the tack room and stable boys

Ortsgruppenführer – local Nazi boss

Ostwall – line of defences built to keep the Red Army out of East Prussia

Panzer – German tank

Rasse und Siedlungshauptamt (RuSHA) – Race and Settlement Office, which screened the ancestry of the brides of SS men in order to 'safeguard the racial purity' of the SS

Hauptsturmführer – SS captain

Reichskommissar –Reich or Imperial Commissioner. During the Third Reich a title given to the Nazi governor of an occupied country

Reichsmarschall – State Marshal, title given to Göring as highest military commander under Hitler

Reichsverteidigungskommissar – Reich or Imperial defence commissioner, an additional title given to Gauleiters making them responsible for civil defence

Remontepräsis – officer in charge of the cavalry's mount-purchasing committee

Schloss – manor house or stately home

Schweike – small, primitive peasant's horse, descendant of wild horses

Stalinorgel – Soviet multiple rocket launchers, known to the Russians as *Katyushas*

Stallmeister – chief groom, or manager, of a stable

Volkssturm – an improvised and barely trained militia founded in October 1944 to augment the Wehrmacht. All males between the ages of 16 and 60 who were not already in some military unit were forced to participate

Wehrmacht – the German armed forces from 1935 to 1945

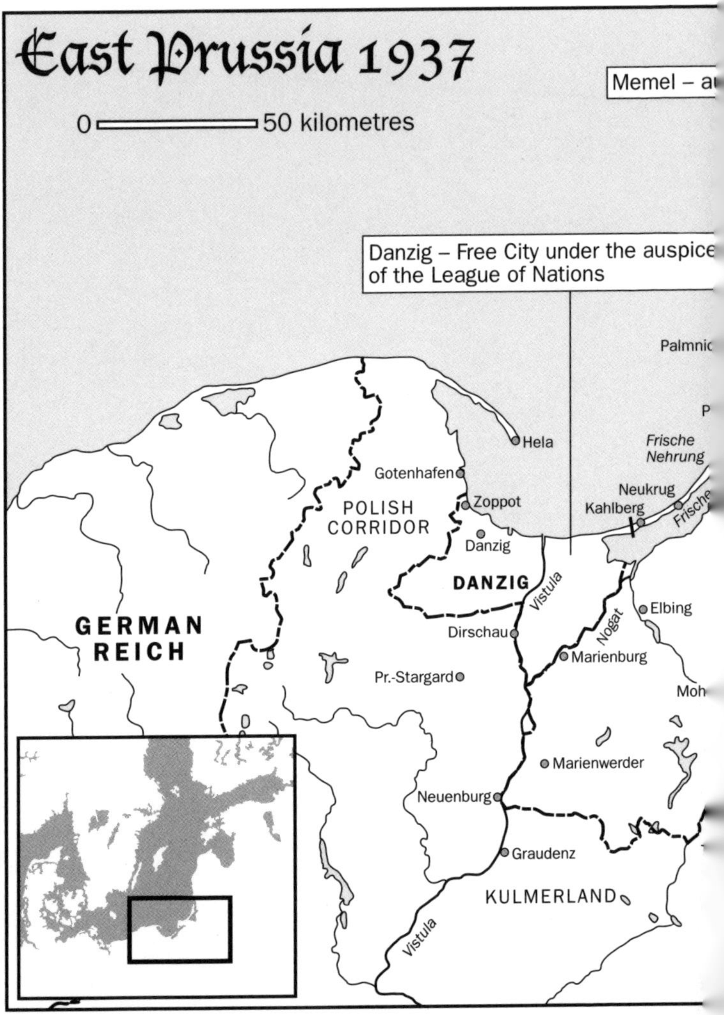

East Prussia 1937
0
50 kilometres
Memel – a
Danzig – Free City under the auspice
of the League of Nations
Palmnic
P
Frische
Nehrung
Hela
Gotenhafen
Zoppot
Neukrug
Kahlberg
Frische
POLISH
CORRIDOR
Danzig
DANZIG
Vistula
Elbing
Nogat
GERMAN
REICH
Dirschau
Marienburg
Pr.-Stargard
Moh
Marienwerder
Neuenburg
Graudenz
KULMERLAND
Vistula

Memel
Schmelz
e 1924
LITHUANIA
Heydekrug
Nidden
Kurische
Nehrung
ssitten
Tauroggen
MEMEL
Ruß
Memel
Tilsit
Ragnit
Lenken
Labiau
D
igsberg
Schloßberg
Ebenrode
(Stallupönen)
Georgenburg
Pregel
Wirballen
Wehlau
Insterburg
Gumbinnen
Trakehnen
MAN
ICH
Angerapp
(Darkehmen)
Tollmingen
r.-Eylau
Gerdauen
Rominten
AST PRUSSIA
Goldap
nstein
Angerburg
sberg
Rastenburg
Bischofstein
Lötzee
Treuburg
Bischofsburg
Lyck
Nikolaiken
enstein
Johannisburg
Ortelsburg
MASUREN
ND

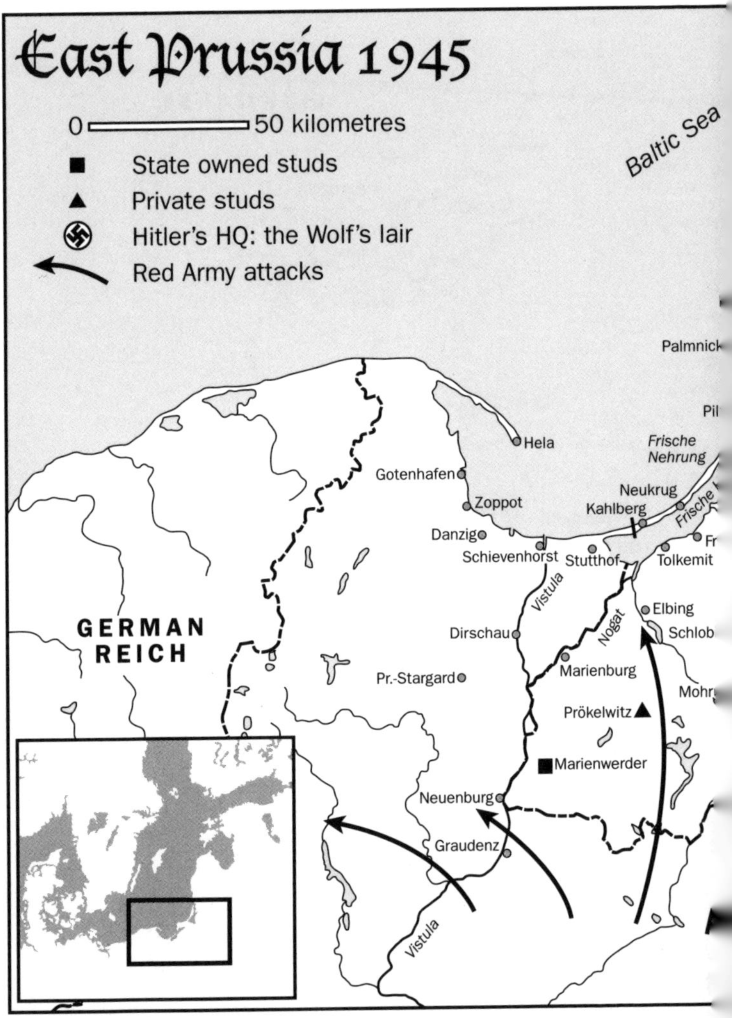
East Prussia 1945
0 50 kilometres
State owned studs
Private studs
Hitler's HQ: the Wolf's lair
Red Army attacks
Baltic Sea
Palmnick
Pil
Hela
Frische Nehrung
Gotenhafen
Zoppot
Neukrug
Kahlberg
Frische
Danzig
Schievenhorst
Stutthof
Tolkemit
Fr
Vistula
Elbing
Schlob
Nogat
Dirschau
GERMAN REICH
Marienburg
Pr.-Stargard
Mohr
Prökelwitz
Marienwerder
Neuenburg
Graudenz
Vistula

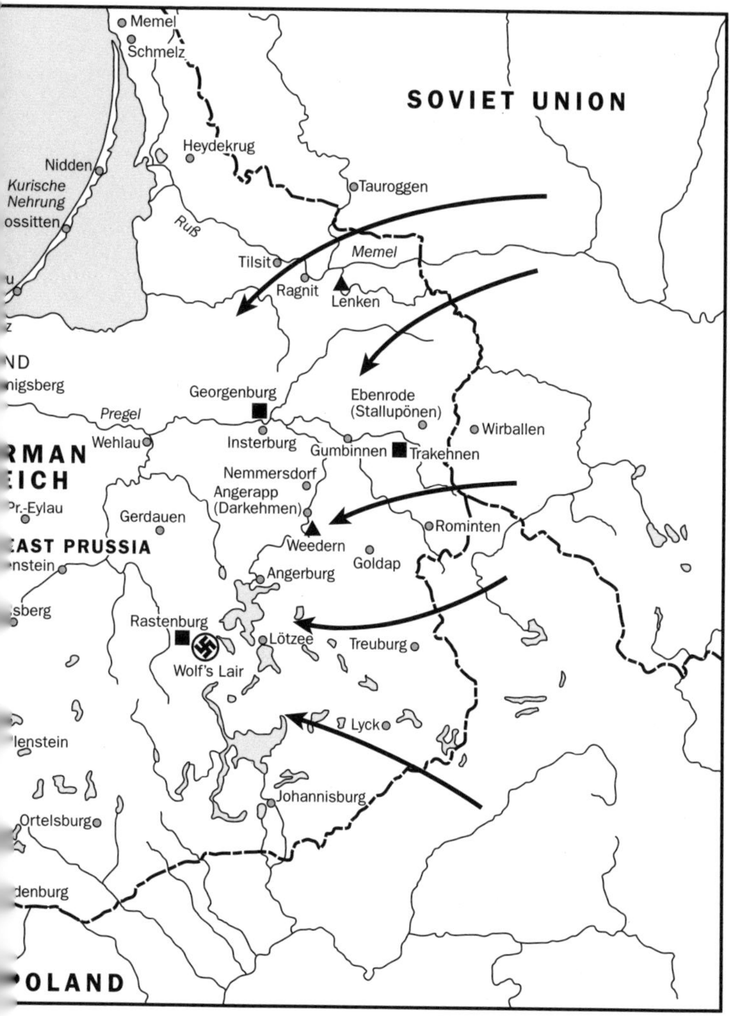

Memel
Schmelz
SOVIET UNION
Heydekrug
Nidden
Kurische
Nehrung
ossitten
Tauroggen
Ruß
Memel
Tilsit
Ragnit
Lenken
ND
nigsberg
Georgenburg
Ebenrode
(Stallupönen)
Pregel
Wirballen
Wehlau
Insterburg
Gumbinnen
Trakehnen
RMAN
EICH
Nemmersdorf
Angerapp
(Darkehmen)
Pr.-Eylau
Gerdauen
Rominten
EAST PRUSSIA
Weedern
Goldap
nstein
Angerburg
sberg
Rastenburg
Lötzee
Treuburg
Wolf's Lair
Lyck
lenstein
Johannisburg
Ortelsburg
denburg
POLAND

Index of Horses

Index of Names